My Thoughts

Kevin Anderson

ISBN 979-8-88945-204-1 (softcover)
ISBN 979-8-88945-205-8 (ebook)

Printed in the United States of America.

Brilliant Books Literary
137 Forest Park Lane Thomasville
North Carolina 27360 USA

Contents

Alone in Love

I remember when I was not alone
I remember when I was happy to be at home
Now I have nothing but regret
Every day is another day I wish I could forget
Love has taken my heart hostage
I'm trapped in a loveless room-marriage
I remember when I was not alone
I remember when I was happy to be at home
My heart once burned with desire
My desire has been doused like a fire
I blame me for the stormy weather
I'm weathering the storm but not forever
I remember when I was not alone
I remember when I was happy to be at home

Am I a Bad Person

Am I a bad person? I have to ask
Am I a bad person because of my past
My life has been a roller-coaster ride
I've been up, down, around, and side to side
Am I a bad person because I want more
Am I a bad person? I want to be rich, not poor
My eyes and my mind want things I can't buy
Stealing them may have crossed my mind, oh my
Am I a bad person? I've lusted and enjoyed sex
Am I a bad person because I love to get wet
My sex, violence, and crimes have pleased me, why
Will I go to heaven after I die
Am I a bad person because life is so unfair
Am I a bad person? I've pretended to care
Why, I'll just ask a very close friend
My gun discharged another's life at an end
Am I a bad person?
My gun is reloaded; the air is clear
Answer the question and be honest; you've nothing to fear

Can You Hear the Silence?

Take a moment to study my walls and my fence
To detect, to delay, and to enhance my defense
They're not made of wood or stone
These barriers are mental, protected by bone
My tongue is a ravenous creature on a leash
My words are used to slay the wildest of beast
It's always on call outside the fence
Can you hear the silence?
This tongue is well trained
On more than one occasion, it's caused great pain
The emotional damage has caused too many rifts
It's caused my relationships to drift
I built the thick walls and the high fence

Can you hear the silence?
My defenses have worked very well
Now, I sit alone in my own mental cell
Can you hear the silence?

A Drink

So life in a drinking man's world is simply a
nibble, a dribble, a sip, and a drip
Hopefully we drinkers can avoid the fourth
stage of life's predestined trip
When all three bottles are empty and the
drip bag is three quarters full
Fill one-quarter drip bag with vodka and ice,
then turn me loose like a raging
bull
One-fourth of my life, I'll nibble
Two-fourth of my life, I'll dribble
Three-fourth of my life, I'll sip
Four-fourth of my life, I'll be raising cane because I refuse to drip
The life of a drinking man is so misunderstood
All drinkers are not drunkards, and in one word, that's good
If life should deal a drinker the drunkard's hand
Have the Clydesdale horse pull the casket for that man
But me—me, I'll refuse the nonalcoholic drip
It not predestined for my last trip
When all three bottles are empty and the
drip bag is three-quarters full
Fill one-quarter drip bag with vodka and ice,
then turn me loose like a raging
bull

Did I Tell U

Some things just go unsaid
Like roses for love are red
Some things are just understood
Like being in love is always good

Some things cannot be explained
Like wanting to endure a loved one's pain
Some things happen out of the blue
Like falling in with a woman like you

Some things are meant to be
Like the relationship between you and me
Some things disrupt, and I do
Did I tell you I love you?

If You Love

The story of love
Some lovers want to be released like a dove
Tethered love will surely die
Unbridled love will soar on high

If you love
It is said that it will come back to you
The boggle is whether or not you want it to
Why was it tethered and wanted to be free
Who changed? You or the lover wanting the flea

If you love
It's one of life's many treasures
Despair lurks within the love chest of pleasures
So if you love someone, set them free
Lovers nest on clouds, not in a tree

If you love
Love only me

I'm Sure She Never Loved Me

I'm sure she never loved me
I'm sure she never cared for us as we
I'm sure I've played the fool for years
I'm sure I've played the clown with tears
I'm sure one warned me not to ask her hand
I'm sure one warned me of her master plan
I'm sure I should've paid attention
I'm sure I should've accepted the intervention
I'm sure not without issues to claim
I'm sure not without a share of the blame
I'm sure love don't love, and that's frightening
I'm sure love don't love, nor does lighting
I'm sure if I had a chance to do it over
I'm sure, if I had, I'd pick a four-leaf clover
I'm sure I'd like to be in love again
I'm sure I'd like to be held by a friend
I'm sure she never cared for us as we
I'm sure she never loved me

Is It Me

Is it me? I've asked myself more than one time
Is it me? You have labeled closed mind?
Is it me? Standing out in the rain?
Is it me? Who culled the blame?
Is it me? I heard it asked
Is it me with the checkered past?
It is I
I'll stand fast
I'll be the one
I'll hold the bag
When the time has come and before it does pass
I'll be marked lest they accuse me
I'll agree
Is it me?

Love and Sorrow

Little Boy Blue,
Who will blow their horn for thee
The lonely heart desires adventure and travel
The vows of love are sealed with a gavel
Little Boy Blue,
Who will blow their horn for thee
Don't ask; for it shall not be me
Little Boy Blue,
Love and sorrow are not separate
Blue, can the power of your horn bifurcate
Little Boy Blue,
Who will blow their horn for thee
Don't ask; for it shall not be me
Sorrow is soured on this mind
Love is unquestionably blind
The putrid matter of sorrow is one's despair
If love were not blind, would it even care
Little Boy Blue,
Who will blow their horn for thee
Don't ask; for it shall not be me

Love Us As We

My love starts with self, then I to me
It branches out from all three
Me, myself, and I are very tight
When we share our love, it's a delight

Don't disrespect me, myself, or I
Our love will turn dark in a blink of an eye
We love to love; we respect to respect
We are a powerful ally or an enemy
beset

If you see me, you need look no further
We're never seen without the other
Give us room to breath
"Don't tread on us" is our creed

Let us be
Love us as we

My First Love Came Home

My life walked out; she said goodbye
She did not really understand why
She waited for me to ask her back
With hurt in my heart, I turned my back

How long is the longest year
Multiply that and count the tears
It's taken a long time for us to come around
We've both grown up; we're both on firm ground

Like duelist, we walked but never looked back
We were headstrong; it's courage we lacked
Our walk came full circle; we're face-to-face
We must have forgotten the dueler's pace

We've no weapons; the fighting is done
We've concluded; neither has won
We've decided we should no longer roam
God has blessed us; my first love came home

No Matter What You Do

No matter what you do
Why does your past haunt you?
Remember when and, oh yes, then
You sit there with a nervous grin

The past is on the hunt again
It happened such a long time ago
You barely remembered, and who would know
You see a face; you hear your name
The past has come to proclaim its fame
Remember when and, oh yes, then

The past is on the hunt again
Every letter and every note you gathered
You destroyed the information that mattered
Could you tell about the incident when?
Okay, explain to me what happened then

You sit there with a nervous grin
The past is the haunt again

One Leaf

It was not too long ago
I wish it wasn't so
A leaf left a tree like a tear dropping into a stream
The tree stood silent; what a dreadful scene
It was the first to turn yellow in the fall
It was proud and the prettiest one of all
It was not too long ago
When the leaf adorned those outstretched arms
It willed itself free into the stream's charm
All the leaves fell, leaving the tree bare
It was not concerned nor chilled by cold air
One leaf was lost; the others were just there
It was not too long ago
Now, I wish it wasn't so
The tree bent over and toppled from the strain
Who'd have known one leaf could cause such pain
From the stream, its leaves grew once again
One willful leaf has never again caused it so much pain

Our House

My heart and my soul are filled with pain
My wife, she's in search of another man
The bonds that tie could not hold the strain
My wife has a blueprint, a divorce plan

My name to her is but ten years of shame
She said our love is a house overdue repair
Nothing can be fixed, and I hold the blame
I'm home alone; she left for fresh air

A house divided, it can't take the strain
Her blueprint, it's the ultimate plan
Goodbye, love, I never meant to cause you pain
My wife, she's in search of another man

The Gift

Packaged it, weighed it, and sealed it closed with a kiss
I sealed the love inside the box, so be careful not to dismiss
I closed my eyes and made a wish
I pressed ever so lightly and not too hard
I didn't dispatch the gift with a letter nor a card

I've expressed myself in word and deed
I refused to attach a letter full of selfish need
Have you ever loved someone sight unseen
Have you ever fell in love with a dream
Say you understand what I mean

You've never seen the air, yet I know you breathe
You've never seen our Lord God, yet I know you believe
I may never hold your delicate hand
I may never size your finger for a band
I have said nothing, but I know you understand

The Warning

This warning is for woman or man
Going through life without a plan
Is your path through life paved with gold
Were you guaranteed to never grow old
Unlike the ant, you set and wait
How can you catch fish without bait
Time keeps ticking; each day goes on
Look at your calendar; a year has gone
Little grasshopper, I've watched you play
Remember, summer's heat will fade one
day
Your house is in need of repair
Winter's nights and days bring very cold
air

This warning is only for you to consider
In old age, you can be happy or bitter
In the summer's heat, it's always warm
In the winter's blizzard, it's always a storm

Time

I guess it's all in a day
The things I do, the things I say
If I stood still, in time, I'd surely fall
When I take a few steps forward, in time, I'd walk into a wall

Time and space are relative
My heart and soul are all I have to give
I guess it's the little things that cause strife
Time leads into time; age matures and seasons life

Time passes from dawn to dust
Time slips into time as it must
A rose seed in time becomes a fully mature rose
Its beauty pleases the eye, and its scent pleases the nose

In time, a diamond is transformed from a piece of coal
Time made it beautiful; time never made it old
You're my rose; you're the beautiful diamond I see
Time and space have brought you closer in time to me

Time II

Twenty-four hours times seven days
So much time has wasted away

Open a time savings account
That could make one rich, no doubt

Father Time is so very cruel
Ticktocks are wasted on fools

No one can save time that is lost
Time is to old age as winter is to frost

Two Ships at Night

Some pass like ships on the ocean at night
You hear me; you know I'm right
How can I express a dream, a wondering, a what-if
What if we commit…and I were to inseminate
What if our intercourse were to escalate
Would life on the ocean be the same
What if I speak out "I love you" with no shame
Don't pass by, Captain; show me your flowing main
I'm on a ship of fools; I should not pursue
But, Captain, how should I approach you
You never signal to me yes or no
You never signal to me to come or go
Why do I choose to run this losing race
Captain, I've pled my case; what did you say, keep in my place
My mind is filled with thoughts of you from whence we met
My eyes tell the story of these lips which I've kept wet
My eyes delight upon seeing your sparkling sight
My lips craved yours for a taste of delight
Friendship and loyalty are a constant plight
Some pass like ships on the ocean at night

Who's Not So Bright?

Today the sun was late
The stars asked it to wait
They shone so bright
They dazzled those in sight

The sun was late today
The moon wanted more time to play
It shone so bright
It amazed onlookers in its brilliant light

Last night, the stars did not shine
The sun found a place to hide
Those stars were not even bright
They could not manifest light

Last night, the moon didn't play
The sun moved its own way
The stars and the moon faced a plight
The sun was heard to say, "Who's not so bright?"

Whose Move Is It

When I think about life
I contemplate the joy and strife
One could compare it chess
Every move should be one's best
The first move, maybe a pawn
An early decision, the morning dawn
Maybe one should have moved the knight
One late decision to contemplate all night
What will the next move be
Calculate the risk and wait for your enemy
Each move changes the game
Each ideal move is hardly the same
The queen is the most powerful piece
Without her, the king may soon be deceased
Chess is a game much like life
Both are compounded with joy and strife
When I think of chess, I think about life

Yesterday, Remember

It's cold now; remember when it was not yesterday?
Winter's night has replaced the noonday's sun.
Remember short nights and long, jubilant days?
Remember summer's warmth and winter's plight?
Remember when day never met night?
Remember why the sky shown blue?
Damn, the day doesn't last as long as it used to.
The sun does not shine as bright.
Remember when memories were such a delight?
Day vacillates night.
Time is measured, January through December.
Gaffers, gammers measure time by what's remembered.
Remember to live in the daylight.
Remember darkness is illuminated by twilight.
The summer has departed, and memories decay.
Gaffers, gammers have inverted sight
It's cold now; who will be warmed by a remembered yesterday?

Thinking of Me

Thank you for thinking of me
Thank you because now I see
Friendship has no bounds
I think of you when you're not around
I often think of you
I'm glad you're thinking of me too
Remember we met by chance
Remember our short romance
It's odd you think of me
It's odd I'd think of we
But, damn, how time moves from dusk to dawn
It seems as if I've just been woken from your yawn
Who'd have thought you were thinking of me
We've come full circle, if measured in degree
I see our friendship will soar past the stars above
I see our friendship is based on love

Sometimes

Sometimes I think it's me
Sometimes I can't see the forest because of the trees
I smile and I laugh when others would surely cry
I smile and I laugh; don't ask me to explain why
When I look in the mirror, I only see me
I've asked myself what others see
Some consider me a waste of usable space
Some consider me a front-runner in life's race
I've looked in the mirror, and I've seen only me
I smile and I laugh at that man staring back at me
Sometimes I think it's me who doesn't know self
Who else would look in the mirror to find themselves

Steadfast

I'm steadfast, who believes in jealous
I have forgiven your shortfalls—please forgive mine
Forgive my pursuit of you, for it is voracious
I've been a sinner since the beginning of time
I've deceived, lied, and lusted, to list a few crimes
I've attempted to change, but I need more time
Will you comfort this weary heart with your soft-spoken words
Can you look into my eyes and see what is said but not heard
I've untied my tongue in order be heard
It was once bound by respect; now it will no longer rest
Let me hold your body and soul tight to my chest
Why talk of passing without a spoken word… That's absurd
God causes the spirit to depart
Man destroys only the flesh and toys with the heart
Ashes to ashes, dust to dust
Our spirits rest with God, not the unjust
No flesh can judge you in any way
You are a loving person forever and always
Do you love me? I ask without shame
Steadfast, not jealous, is my name

You Asked

How can a person be so sweet
How can I describe such a treat
How come your love shines brighter than the sun
How, it's because you're second to none

When did I realize I was in love with you
When did one plus one equals anything but two
When I wake, I say your name
When I go to sleep, I do the same

Why do I feel our love is true
Why, it's because our hearts are bonded with super glue
Why do our hearts beat as one, not two
Why, it's because Cupid's arrow has run us through

Where does our love take us from here
Wherever we desire, my dear
Where can you find someone who loves you like me
Where oh where could such a person be

Run Life's Race

Run life's race as fast as you can
Don't look over your shoulder again
Always keep one eye on the prize
Beware of smiling face ; they sometimes tell lies

Remember to take a breath and adjust your speed
Run hard and strong just like a steed
Being first to finish the race is your goal
You'll stand in the winner's circle with that medal of gold
How does it feel to be the first one
Do you think it's over because you have won

Beware of the handshake, a pat on the back
That hand may be the one to push you offtrack
There are no winners; the race is never won
Put on your best sneakers; get ready to run

Don't Stop

Why did you stop
Did it take too long to reach the top
Was the bar you set too high
Did you reach for a star but never reached the sky

Why did you give up so soon
Did your visions of glory end at noon
Was the battle you chose destined for defeat
Did your dreams get dashed to your feet

Why did you let go of hope
Why didn't you pull instead of push the rope
Was the path you choose overgrown and your way unclear
Did you lose your way because of fear

Take his hand—walk with me
Take these glasses—they'll help you see
Take this road map—it shows the way
Take your dreams to the Almighty—every day

Will We Be More

When will we be more than true friends
We have discussed life's being till life's end
What can I do—where do I begin
Will we ever be lovers or just true friends

I remember my feelings—you remember yours too
I'm here, and you're there—what should I do
Didn't I tell you—I love you

When I talk to you—I'm smiling through the phone
True friends or lovers—should not be alone
When I think about us, I wish we shared a home
It would be filled with love—its roof would be a dome

I sit here questioning if we'll be more
I sit here wondering and praying you'll open that door
I'd rise with open arms to embrace and adore
I'll continue to love as a true friend—this I can assure

Can You Feel Me

I will always inform you as to how I feel
Just to remind you my love is real
Romeo said, "Let me count the ways"
His words were eloquent, but I will say

If life were a flower garden, you'd be a rose
Out of all the flowers, you're the one I chose
Believe in my intentions because they're true
Pay me attention; it's the only surcharge due

The blind can see the way I feel in the air
The deaf can hear the way I feel everywhere
These feelings are special and one of a kind
These feeling are malignant; they're not benign

Everything has a substitute but not for thee
Sweet'N Low is a sugar but not for me
You are sweeter than the sugar in my tea
With trust and respect, you can believe in we

My Seeds

My seeds have sprouted, and I'm very proud, you know
They are branching out, and their leaves have begun to grow
I pray they will bear good fruit
I pray they have embedded well their root

They'll be honored as the mightiest of trees
They'll grow independent; they'll surely succeed
They'll be shelters, providers of shade
I'm just the humble gardener, whose love will never fade

It Happened to Me

I remember when it happened to me
I've got the scars; want to see
I was young and on the run
Forever on the search for fun

It really doesn't seem too long ago
The scars have healed, you know
Well, it hurt, but now there's no pain
I kept my head up and my eyes on the game

Well, I'm better now in spite of it all
Me, I'm in it for the long haul
Every moment and every step, I'll not forget
Not a day was a day to regret

I understand something similar happened to you
Well, keep your eyes open and your ears too
I remember when it happened to me
I have the scars; do you want to see

The Snake

There's a good reason for binocular vision
To track and to make precise judgment decisions
The challenge is whether to strike the body or the mind
Without binocular vision, decisions are made blind

Speed, surprise, and violence are my actions
Indiscriminate assaults are momentary satisfactions
Wit, cunning, and knowledge are subject based
The first strike is always the face

Observation can come from above or below
Where the attack will come from, only the snake will know
Beware of how you approach me
Camouflage and stealth make me difficult to see

Don't think yourself superior to the snake
Be careful not to make that fatal mistake
Snake hunters and the like, heed the warning—steer clear
I walk upright; I stand tall without fear

Pillars of Stone

We're just flesh and bone
Together, we stand like pillars of stone
Life has weathered our young face
We've weathered life with amazing grace

We've survived summer's heat and winter's cold
Our triumphs helped us to stand so proud and so bold
Marked by vandals who left us battered and chipped
Undermined where we stand, but our foundation never slipped

High winds of change, gust so hard
We've never toppled like a house of cards
Rain splattered and dripped down our face
The tracks of our tears can't be traced

Together, we hold the weight of the world
Like sand in a clam's mouth, our love formed is a pearl
We're just flesh and bone
Together we stand like pillars of stone

Can I See It

Did you hear what she said to me
She asked me over so I could see
I can't image what it looks like
I'm sure it will be quite a sight

I'm going to see; I have my doubts
I want to see what she's talking about
She's really anxious for me to see
I wonder if she'll give it to me

You know I've never seen one
What's going to happen when we're done
She might let me touch it
She said no one's ever been bit

Did you hear what she said
I saw your face turn red
Please don't say that it's dumb
I'm going to see her rabbit chew gum

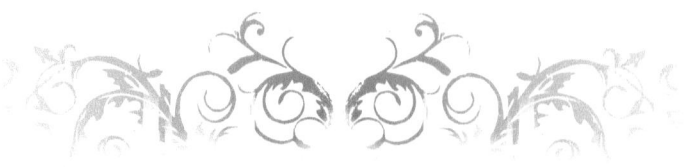

Love and Trust

If love were candy, trust would make it sweet
Love and trust together make life a joyous treat
If love were a melody, you'd surely tap your feet
Ears would beat their drums; the heart would pump its beat

Love without sweetener and music is unjust
Love is sour and toneless without trust
To say "I love you," caveat, but "I don't trust you" strikes a fatal cut

Trust is the sweetener, the melody on which love strives
Without candy and music, love will not survive
Love and trust together make candy so sweet
Love and trust together make a musical beat

If love and trust were the only treats
The menu would read "All you can eat"
Love without trust is a sour tart
Love and trust together are candy and music for the heart

The Wall

The writing was on the wall
Was it written outside or in the hall
I've never seen it, but I've heard it said
The message on the wall was written in red

I must have missed it; I didn't see
Why didn't anyone inform me
Was it that obvious
Red writing is somewhat conspicuous

Who wrote the warning of impending disaster
What did it say: slow down or go faster
Who's in charge of this mysterious wall
Please have the author give me a call

I'm going to inform him or her of how it's so unfair
To leave my messages on a wall somewhere
So next time just give me a call
And to stop writing my messages on the wall

Good Morning!

Good morning! How was your sleep
I lay awake most of the night counting sheep
Where did your dreams take you
I saw you tossing the whole night through

As I lay to rest, you laid your arm across my chest
I vow to be your best
I'll be your best friend
I'll be your best lover till the end

I'll be your best provider
I'll fulfill your every desire
I fell asleep and dreamed of you
Sleeping on a cloud, sipping honeydew

Dancing on a sunbeam in the sunlight
Without a worry or concern for the night
Good morning! How was your sleep
I lay awake most of the night counting sheep

Life Passed Me By

While sitting and watching out my window
I wondered why grass grows so slow
Does every blade have a story to tell
Freshly cut grass has a wonderful smell

While sitting and watching, I saw a bird fly by
I wonder what it's seen on high
How does it feel to soar in the wind
I'd soar up and down, then do it again

While sitting and watching, I saw a cloud
It floated away into a cloud crowd
It was all fluffy and quite unique
It appeared to be shaped in the form of a beak

While sitting and watching, life passed me by
Plants, animals, and clouds in the sky
While sitting and watching, all I really wanted to know
How long must I sit and watch to see the grass grow

She Knows

I did not have to say a thing
I watched her move, her hips swing
Her eyes appeared to catch my glow
She turned away, but I know she knows

She knows she's a lady who turns heads
She knows most men desire to bed
She knows the days and nights are hers
She knows most men would buy her furs

I think she is the fountain of youth
Just one kiss would reveal the truth
With her passion, I'd never be cold
With her embrace, I'd never grow old

She knows she has turned my head
Her hips hypnotize without a word said
Her smile warms me all over, and I glow
I'm on fire, and I know she knows

The Mission

Where are we going if we have no vision
More and more, I perceive minor division
Some days we get sidetracked by unimportant facts
Some days we attempt to control how the other one acts

Without our dreams, there's no vision
We claim to have dreams; let's make a few decisions
Let's not let naysayers cause us to fight
Let's stand hand in hand; let's do what's right

Let's not let the weather darken our blue skies
Let's not let nightfall cause our dreams to die
There'll be roadblocks and detours in our path
Like the problem solvers we are, we'll do the math

We do have dreams and a vision
We must stand together in decision
Let no one create doubt or division
Let's make our lives together our primary mission

Take a Chance

Are you willing to take a chance
On life, on love, and on true romance
I'm willing to take a risk
To live and to love is bliss

Toss a coin and without fail
Fifty percent of the time, it's heads or tails
I'll make a bet…no, a pledge
One-third of the time, it will land on edge

The odds are two to one
Without betting on the edge, life is no fun
The third dimension is our reality
Count the sides—one, two, and three

Take a chance on life, on love, and on true romance
I'm more than willing to take that chance
On the edge is where we ought to be
Take a chance on love, on you, and on me

Lady Bird

I remember how about you
She helped me along as I grow
She taught me the most important things
Like, after every winter, in comes spring

She taught me how to lace and to tie my own shoes
She taught me that, in life, we all pay dues
The hardest lessons were followed by a loving kiss
She encouraged my dreams with a good wish

Most of all, she taught me to see
Beyond the forest and through the trees
Like a bird, she built our nest
When I flew away, she had done her best

She taught me how to fly
She believed in me; she encouraged me to give it a try
She is a Lady Bird like no other
I want everyone to know I love my mother

Between the Lines

Because you're seated at the table doesn't mean you'll dine
Learn to read between the lines
I'm weary of those familiar words
The real message often goes unheard

Learn to decipher the double-talk
Does "Move forward" mean to run or walk
Did "Do it the best way you can"
Mean delegate it to the next man

Is communication a word game
How can yes and no mean the same
Do you mind if I sit here
No! But I'd rather you not sit so near

Could you say what you said again
Start at the end and then begin
Is everyone seated ready to dine
Only eat what's yours because all of the food is mine

All Mine

My favorite place is in your arms
Being caressed like a lucky charm
My heart and soul are yours to hold
Treasure them like a pot of gold

When your lips are softly pressed to mine
I'm drunk off love; it's like wine
One step forward and two steps back
Kiss me again, just one good smack

You're the one, more precious than stones
Rubies, diamonds, or ivory bones
More desirable, more beautiful, more adored
Being without you, I can't afford

I long to be in my favorite place
In your arms, affectionately admiring your face
Kissing those luscious lips, filled with wine
You're the one; you're all mine

Action or Inaction

For every action or inaction
There's an equal or greater reaction
A dropped stone caused the water to ripple
Cause and effect isn't really that simple

A chance meeting, an alluring glance
The summer's heat, a sizzling romance
One day leads into the next
Is this a blessing or a cruel hex

Days have led to months; is it true
Those three words: I love you
Do you love me, awaiting a reply
On this true day, the relationship may live or die

Months have led to years of happiness or tears
Either loving touches or contempt laced with fear
The dropping of a stone caused the ripple effect
Action or inaction, it's time to elect

Can I Help

Can I help you back on your feet
It appears you have fallen on your seat
Let's walk together up this slope
At the top of the hill, there's hope

Can I help you get underway
Let's take small steps, maybe one a day
You know down and out isn't the place to be
Don't be counted out: one, two, three

Can I help you on your plan
I'm willing and able to lend you a hand
My back and shoulders are very wide
I'll share the burden; get on, let's ride

Can I help you clear your path
I'll clear the way; you take a bath
Wash away the tears; clean your mind of fears
I'm here for you; your path is clear

The Big City

Life in the big city
It sure is nice, but it ain't real pretty
The bright city lights cast a wonderful glow
The smog chokes, and the traffic is slow

Life in the big city
It sure is nice, but it ain't real pretty
Buildings jammed and stacked side by side
Nature thrown out, taken on a fatal ride

Life in the big city
It sure is nice, but it ain't real pretty
People and rats watch the other grow
Both are killers; who done it, no one knows

Life in the big city
It sure is nice, but it ain't real pretty
Where else would I even think to live
Death and overcrowding—it has so much to give

Treasure

I didn't really lie—about having a throne
I am a king; I wasn't really wrong
My house is my castle, my kingdom, my home
My crown is my head, often referred to as a dome

The hundreds of horses that I race and keep
Those horses are kept under the hood of my jeep
Most of the places I said we'll see
Well, I do have a satellite TV

The masses that stand for my review
Well, that's the grass covered by dew
The flower gardens lined up in rows
That garden produced a single rose

I never lied about my wealth or treasure
My heart and soul are here for your pleasure
This treasure is all I really want you to see
It's the love shared between you and me

What's Different

What's different this time around
Ringling Brothers has fewer clowns
Under the big top where fools showcase
We've left all those clowns in that place

Acting a fool for others who laugh last
Being a fool for others is all in the past
We refuse to paint on a fake red smile
Playing the clown isn't our style

Everybody is somebody's fool
Let's be the exception to the rule
Let's stay away from suspicion and distrust
Communication and understanding are a must

Clowns are never up for this task
Neither of us will ever wear a clown's mask
Respect, love, and trust are a must, you know
We'll never be a part of the big-top show

Comfort

Comfort is a place or a state of mind
It's plentiful and scarce; it's hard to find
It's a place where worry and pain are forgotten
It's a state where peace of mind isn't spoiled or rotten

Life is served hot or too cold to hold
Sometimes it's served on a plate, sometimes in a bowl
It's comfortable when served lukewarm
But there's always a calm before the storm

Comfort isn't always a place to rest
It's a state of mind, knowing you've done your best
Comfort isn't always a state of mind
It's a place where love and trust can shine

Comfort is in your embrace
Your look, your smile, your loving face
Comfort is a place or a state of mind
Our love is comfort forever intertwined

Playing the Odds

Life is not a game of cards
Or a roll of the dice—looking for the hard
If you leave everything to chance
Your fortune could be won or lost in a glance

Betting for or against the odds
Rubbing on a Buddha or praying to God
Laying it all out on the line
Hoping or praying everything will be fine

Some play with a cold, hard poker face
While waiting to be dealt that last ace
Some roll the dice, betting on the hard eight
Shaking and blowing hot air on the hands of faith

Put away the cards and dice
Plan for the future; think about this twice
Take charge; grab life by the horns today
One bad hand or roll will end your play

The Path

The path I walk, I walk alone
The choices I make aren't always condoned
Too often I have to pick and choose
The choices aren't always win or lose

To walk my path is a must
Along the way, I attempt to do what's right and just
Others seek to judge me as I walk
I've learned to listen more than I talk

I'm alone but not lost
Every step I take, I must pay the cost
I'm confused sometimes, and I walk in doubt
I've learned to live with, and I've learned to live without

The path I walk is through life, in my mind
The wide path I avoid and the narrow path I struggle to find
On my path are my dreams and my visions
My path is littered with my expectations and my decisions

Reflection

I recall the day we met
I remember my palms were wet
My world I wanted you in
We laughed and joked; we begin

We tested the limits and made our plans
We ran around town holding hands
The questions asked were about you
I'm sure the questions asked were about me too

I did not think I'd fall so hard
On my heart, I'd posted a guard
I dismissed the guard because of your distraction
My unguarded heart filled quickly with passion

I will never regret the day we met
We're more than a couple; we're a set
Together there's no mountain too high to climb
I'll share your burdens; will you share mine

Forgive Me

First of all, I apologize
For causing tears to fall from your eyes
I abused the trust you had in me
Now, I'm the last person you wish to see

Forgive me for the pain I caused
The loss of your trust has given me pause
I've paused to look deep within
My actions caused me to lose a valued friend

I'm a shattered man
Without you to hold my hand
Every day I miss your touch
Is asking your forgiveness too much

From deep within, I make this plea
Please restore your trust in and forgive me
First of all, I apologize
For causing tears to fall from your lovely eye

Forgive Me II

I poured the tears from your lovely eyes
Your hurt consumed me, the shock, the surprise
I never, ever thought it would be
Those tears rushed out all over me

I felt detached from the human race
I bowed my head; I suffered disgrace
The hurt I caused does and will end
With love and trust, the healing can begin

With you alone, my heart, I share
Wipe away your tears; believe I do care
I refused to drown in your tears and my sorrow
Life is for living; there's always a tomorrow

Dry those tears like the sun dries rain
Let your heart heal; abandon your pain
When fear and distrust resided inside one's heart
No amount of love and trust can heal a world torn apart

On the Brink

On the brink, my life began
On the brink, I know it will end
I stand on the edge of tomorrow
On the brink, there's both love and sorrow

The slope is steep on the leeward side of the brink
There's no time for indecision; ponder, think
Looking up the slope, the top is so blurry
The gravity of it all pulls so hard I worry

On the brink, trumpets may not sound
Doubts and confusion can compound
I'm standing on the brink of it all
With strong legs and good balance, I will not fall

On the brink is where life gives its hardest test
On the brink, only the weary of mind and heart find rest
Every day I stand on the brink
Success is a contract written in erasable ink

The Assassin

Passion is a flame burning out of control
Distrust is a killer who's always on patrol
Bleeding hearts are cold and filled with fear
Distrust killed the passion with a single tear

When the laughter died, how did it go
Tear-crowded eyes which drip drop to a flow
Passion and laughter died; they left a frown
A strong heart can turn distrust around

Laughter will sound again and fill the air
Passion rekindled hotter and more sincere
The assassin lurks in a weak heart that cares
Strong hearts burn forever without despair

One fire is lit; one fire fades away
Love and trust conquer distrust—just pray
Faded laughter, teardrops, and hearts without passion
Distrust is the culprit; it's the assassin

On Bended Knees

How can I truly be to please
Should I bow or come to you on bended knees
I've made so many mistakes
Every decision is one made too late

Is there a way to show I care
Life without you is so unfair
We melt into each other like hot balls of wax
Our passion is nothing more than a fact

Please don't ever take your heart from me
I'm lost without you; can't you see
How did we get so caught up in this
I've tossed a penny into the well, and it's for you I wish

Listen because I'm for real
The obstacles we face, we both can deal
The time we share is heaven-sent
I'll bow to you; know my knees are bent

Lights Out

I've taken the world in my hands without shame
And I've never danced to the cheers of the crowd
But I love to hear the last breath; it's so loud

I have; have you ever turned out the light
The dark rushes in; it's quite a delight
The pupils expand to question why
It's so dark; did the light have to die

Crimson shades and dark secrets; let's share
Darkness and blood fill the air
A flickering candlelight could spell doom
If the slightest breeze blows through the room

The last thing I'll allow you to see
Is my smiling face, a dim vision of me
Everyone will know my name
When the time comes, I'll come without shame

On My Mind

If I could think of something else, I don't think I would
That's not something I think I could
You crowd every corner of my mind
If I were forbidden to see you, I'd rather be blind

I feel your presence when you're not here
I reminisce about holding you near
Your touch, your word, your loving atmosphere
With my whole being, I need you, my dear

The saying is "All good things must come to an end"
The fire burning in my heart only burns over and over again
We're like a circle; where do we begin
Our destiny has yet to be written

If I could think of something else
It would not be of self
I'd think only of what you mean to me
I know you are an important part of my destiny

Good Morning, Mrs. V.

Good morning, Mrs. V. How did you sleep?
I spent most of my night counting sheep
I listen to the night's wind blow
I dreamed you warmed me; did it snow?
Good morning, Mrs. V. How did you sleep?
I stayed awake most of the night counting sheep
I thought about seeing you soon
I dreamed we walked in the light of a full moon
Good morning, Mrs. V. How did you sleep?
I looked out of the window while counting sheep
I wished upon a shining star
I dreamed I was there where you are
Good morning, Mrs. V. How did you sleep?
I woke up this morning thinking about counting sheep
I had the biggest smile on my face
I dreamed about warm snow, about moonlight,
and about your amazing grace

Rising Son

My son warms my heart and brightens my every day
He keeps me on the right path; he's the reason I don't stray
I'm nothing more than a speckle, straining a grain of sand
I'm the speckle who must influence my son who will soon be a man
His love for me is boundless
For me, he does his best
His hero is not a superman with an *S* embroidered on his chest
I'm his hero, his daddy who must straighten out any mess
One day, he'll know I'm not the smartest man in the world
He'll really figure this out when we talk about girls
How will I explain the opposite sex
I've loved and lost, lost and loved; it's all been a hex
I'll tell him a woman is flesh of your flesh, bone of your bone
A woman is your companion; she keeps you from being alone
My son will grow to be wise, proud, and strong
In Jesus' name, I pray to God; I don't steer
my pride and my joy wrong

Behind These Words

Can you feel the meaning behind these words?
As a realist, I face myself.
I ask myself: Who am I? Where am I going?
How will I get there? When will I know if I have arrived?
As I take my journey through life, I stop
along the path to smell the flowers;
I take time to soak my feet in the ponds, rivers,
streams, and oceans along the way.

I have loved, and I have been loved;
I have befriended, and I have been befriended;
I have weathered the storms, and I have enjoyed
the sunrise time and time again.

Can you feel the meaning of these words that illuminated my path?
My path is narrow; it has depth; it has way stations along the way.
At each way station, there's a mirror for
reflection and a light for illumination.
Can you feel the meaning behind these words?

Too Much

I can't understand why I feel
Our love for one another is surreal
I'm lost without your touch
Can I love you too much

I think of you; I can't sleep at night
I toss and turn; I long for a glimpse or sight
Our lives are forever intertwined
Passion and love carefully mixed or combined

I think about the first day we met
I think about our body heat, our sweat
Pressed so tightly into the other's arms
Savoring the taste of the other's charm

I can't explain the way I feel
But I can assure you: my love is for real
I'll never recover from your touch
My love for you is not too much

From Biology to History

I felt your presence while learning biology
While being taught about what makes us we
You sat with pen in hand
Paying close attention to another man

How I wished you were listening to me
Not that teacher talking on and on endlessly
I thought about touching your hand
I formulated a master plan

A bold introduction, I'd risk it all
Here are my, digits give me a call
I need help in class
My opportunity to make my pass

But I never acted decisively
Today we sit in history
I remember my plan from biology
Risk it all; give me a call, acting decisively

Who's Driving

I heard you when you first drove up
You're in tow; you're hitched; I shan't interrupt
Even though our feelings are real
You're out of the race; no one's at the wheel

I'm pleased we've breached the other's world
Acknowledging romantic desires between a boy and a girl
I'll pump my brakes; I've been known to move fast
I can image a beautiful future; I feel our friendship will last

You've duly informed me of that band of gold
But if there's nothing there, why should you hold
Onto a symbolic band that's broken and tattered
I'll question no more; it should not matter

I'm a driver; I'm in control; we're face-to-face
You've waved the yellow flag; I'm out the race
I heard you when you first drove up
You're in tow; you're hitched; I shan't interrupt

Perception, Not Deception

I'm not as cunning as you perceive
I've been straightforward in order not to deceive
We dance our dance at your speed
I'm only able or allowed to give you what you feel you need
I'm not jumping from lay to lay
I'm not a scorekeeper; I'm not keeping a play by play
You're an influential and alluring person
per se, who came into my life
Our timing may not be perfect, thereby causing you emotional strife
You're not meant to be discarded, used, or labeled obsolete
You have my nose wide open; you've caused
my heart to pause, to skip a beat
Your perception of me isn't worth its weight in gold
My pledge is no deception; it's a pledge I wish to uphold
I'm not selfless; I'm willing to suffer in our despair
You're the breath in my lungs; you're my fresh air
You can use me as you will
I'll ensure you get your proper fill
You're true to my heart, okay
And in my heart, you will stay

Do You See What I See

Do you see what I see
Me, I'm a mountain; and you, you're the ocean and the sea
Look beyond the horizon; the sun has been
set free from beyond your sea
Heating the ocean and the mountain on which life depends
My majestic mountain precariously sliding into your ocean
Do you see what I see
Our hearts radiating heat between you and me
Do you see the sun setting between our eyes
Do you feel the heat radiating between our thighs
Do you see what I see
Steam from hot springs radiating joy and glee
Our desires burning hotter than the sun
Our obstacles, small hurdles to be overrun
Do you see what I see
Me, I'm a mountain; and you, you're the ocean and the sea
Beyond the horizon, the sun set free from the sea
Radiating heat which our lives depend
The majestic mountain slid into the ocean

The Blueprint

I woke up this morning with a smile
Even though I would not see you for a while
The first thing I do is reach for the phone
Hoping and praying you'll be at home

Every time your phone ringer rings
My anticipation and desperation grows—I cling
My body and my mind collide until you answer the phone
Your voice gently caresses my ear to the bone

Let's draft our blueprints for our dreams
Over two cups of hot water, sugar, mixed with coffee and cream
Let's go over our visions while eating grapes and sipping wine
Let's go over our blueprint line by line

When we wake up tomorrow, we won't need a phone
Our blueprint will ensure we're no longer alone
We'll review our dreams and visions every year
We'll review our blueprint; our love will ring in our ear

Sunshine

You're a beautiful woman, and you'll forever be my girl
You are my sunshine; you illuminate my world
During my darkest nights, I think of you
Your loving and caring ways turn my gray sky blue

Time and space keep me from my heart
Life has found a way to keep us apart
With all of me, I hope and pray
Our time and space will come together one day

I can envision us holding hands
Laughing and playing while making plans
We comfort each other when the lights are down
We console each other when our tears turn our smiles to frowns

You are my sunshine, forever bright
My safe way through my darkest night
You turn my gray sky blue
You're my heart, and I love you

Fate or Faith

The path I took was not straight
At the fork in the road, I embark by fate
I walked around the obstacles, over, never
It took me a long time, but me, me, I was clever
I sold Eskimos flip-flops
Made Little Bo Peep sell her sheep for a few lollipops
I was there when Gimme got drowned in a soda pop bottle
I remember when "What's ya name" followed
"Puddin' Tane" full throttle
I was there when she was born, you know
My world changed as I watched her grow
She cries for a chance to be held in my arms
I'll let nothing in this world do her harm
She turns my world from left to right
She laughs; she cries; she keeps me up all night
The path I take is more than straight
At the fork in the road, I embark by faith

Pilot to Copilot

Much like air traffic control clear pilot and copilot to land
Communication between them must be easy to understand
The tower sent mixed messages, saying we're all clear
As seasoned pilots, we both have our fear

We want to land; experience tells us not here
Let's keep our wits about us and retract the landing gear
As long as we keep this relationship aloft
We'll use fluffy clouds as pillows, so light and so soft

We're traveling through uncertain time and uncharted space
While flying high, let's keep talking with a smile on our face
One day, we'll have to land this relationship
Let's land on solid ground so we've not wasted a trip

Not every relationship is ready to land
"Pilot to copilot, are we there yet?" asked a woman to a man
Mixed messages from the tower may say to proceed
Communication is an important factor
for our relationship to succeed

In My Corner

In my corner, she stood
As we battle life's issues as only we could
We face life toe-to-toe
We absorb its punches blow by blow

In my corner, she stood
Like no other woman would
Sweat and blood canvas our face
She angelically strokes away my shame, my disgrace

In my corner, she stood
Even when my intentions were no good
With a smile and a kiss, she'd interject
With stern words and passion, she'd correct

She's my lady; she's definitely all in
She's my support; she's my best friend
In our corner, we make our grandstand
She's my woman; and me, me, I'm her man

Where

On the other side of nowhere, somewhere resides
One can get there if you crawl, walk, run, or ride
From nowhere to somewhere is circumspect
To leave nowhere is impossible at best

To leave from somewhere is quite possible
However, to end up nowhere is very probable
Considering this, let me retract
To leave from nowhere from somewhere is a fact

Nowhere and somewhere are one and the same
Somewhere is nowhere; it's all in a name
One often goes nowhere pretty damn fast
Even though one will end up somewhere at last

When your travels take you to where
Take note of the scenery; take in some fresh air
On the other side of nowhere, somewhere resides
One can get there if you crawl, walk, run, or ride

My Baby Girls

Racheal and Marquettah, you are my world
You're my daughters; my baby girls
Excuses, time, and distance—three degrees
from outright persistence

The three have kept us a world apart
Not one day forgotten, you are my heart
Excuses, time, and distance robbed me of your kiss
Without your hugs, your touches left my heart amiss

I'm your father; I'm your daddy, a picture on the wall
My face is familiar; my voice, a phone call
I can't turn back the hands of time
Money can't replace me no matter how shiny the dime

Marquettah and Racheal, you are my heart and my soul
To me, you are more precious than gold
I love you; you're daddy's baby girls
No more excuses, time, and distance in our world

The Four Chambers

My heart is protected by flesh and bone
You crushed it with silence; you left me alone
I search its four chambers for a glimpse or two
It's dark and gloomy in there without you

Respect, trust, honesty, and love are on its walls
Each chamber is empty; it echoes as I call
Baby girl, baby girl, come back to me please
Your silence is a burden; it has brought me to my knees

My candle, I've lit from both ends
It can't illuminate the four chambers within
Too soon, it will burn out without your touch
Please come back to me; am I asking too much

My heart is now unprotected by flesh and bone
You walked out; your silence left me alone
Please don't walk out and leave me in the dark
Illuminate these four chambers; light up my heart

No Mr. Anderson

Good to hear you're in good cheer
I make you laugh aloud from afar, not near
Deep within, I understand
You want to be married; you're looking for a good man

I haven't seen you since we met
Mr. Anderson—he's your cat; he's your pet
Through your cat's eyes, I can't see you, my dear
Circumstances, my issues have made that clear

I guess you've concluded I'm not the one for you
I can't fulfill your honey do
No pressure or regret
Not making time for me, I can respect

Just think of me from time to time
It's a pleasure just to be on your mind
There will always be a fire burning—true
Kindled by forbidden thoughts of you

Hot and Dangerous

Some like it extremely hot and dangerous
When you touch my fire, you must be very courageous
Some climb the highest mountains, and others dive the deepest seas
Both acts are dangerous, and the courageous
level—twenty thousand leagues

While you're in my web, you may find it hard to leave
It's a little sticky, and it's a tangled web I weave
We're both behind the wheel, but only one of us can drive
Let go; I'm blind, but I'll keep us both alive

I'll push the clutch; you shift the gear
It's an automatic, but I like you near
The warning reads "Slippery when wet"
What are you waiting for; slide it into first—bet

Labored sweat under red-hot flaming candles
Dripping wet, melting hot wax on love handles
Some like it extremely hot and dangerous
Could that same some be referring to us

Don't Confuse Me

I pour out feeling from my heart like water
into your cup; I hope to fill
I feel beyond sexual pleasures that momentary thrill
Me, I'm an admiral of a fleet of failed relationships
You should take precaution and avoid
taking a dreadful, pleasurable trip

Please don't—I'll say again—don't get caught up in my wake
I have too many issues; stay clear for your own sake
You are a beautiful woman, a true Nubian queen
The web I weave is heartbreak; no, it's
pleasure or something in between

Don't attempt to change me via your "You
should be more like" mold
Fresh Play-Doh is for youngsters; me, me, I'm too old
When you look at me, see me for who I am
Don't confuse me with jelly; baby girl, I'm jam

Let me tell you the rest of the story about Jack and Jill
Most think it was an accident, him falling down that hill
Jill insisted Jack be more like Humpty Dumpy, you may recall
Jack was not confused, so to end it, he took that fatal fall

Good Night

Good night, love; sleep without fear
I'm here to whisper words of encouragement in your ear
Good night, sweetheart; I'm praying for you on bended knees
I pray life willfully fulfill your every need

Close your eyes; let your mind be at ease
Tomorrow awaits you with sunshine and a cool morning breeze
It's lost without your yawn
Without you, the day could not end; the morn could not dawn

Good night, love; sleep in heavenly bliss
Life will fulfill your every wish
Good night, sweetheart; I'm praying for you every day
I pray nothing in life will stand your way

Close your eyes; let your mind roam free
Tomorrow awaits you with honeysuckle, morning dew, and me
The night seems long, but it only lasts a little while
Good night; tomorrow and I await your touch and your smile

Wow

Wow says we can be all we should be
Wow is a word that sounds so sexy
Wow is all you can say
Wow is a mouthful for one day

I can come up with more words; I'll say a few
Let's mix the letters of our alphabet stew
Lovely, passionate, and debonair
Clear and not cloudy, a breath of fresh air

Can you feel the weight of two
It's heavy yet lighter than morning dew
You carry it around, yet no one knows it but you
Concealing our weight, what will you do

Wow…all I can say is wow
Wow is a word you can feel now
Wow is all you can say
Wow is a mouthful for one day

Future Vet

There's a tear in my eye; I've faced death but did not die
I got up today without regret
I proudly donned my dark-blue beret

Serving this country with total respect
Bloodstained uniforms, half the country rejects
I can't choose the cause, but I fight for a way
Freedom is my choice, my voice; I fight for your say

Freedom is everything but free
The tear in my eye is for those who can't see
I don't make policy; I don't make beliefs
I don my beret to prevent future grief

I did not face the face of death alone
Blood-soaked uniforms will never see home
No one has spit on me as of yet
But one day soon, I'll be a vet

When I'm in Her Presence

When I'm in her presence, her aura licks like a perpetual flame
Her heat is so intense the sun is a shame
Like a candle, I'm melting; I'm liquefying; I'm wax dipping to a flow
When I'm in her presence, I wish the wind would blow
Have you met her; could you know
Watch my eyes; you'll see the fire; look closely…you'll see my glow
Her fire burns inside me, and I want her more
An ocean is between us; her heat warms my shore
When I'm in her presence, her voice sings
I hear music; what's that, a diamond ring
How many karats; how many do you think
Too many is enough; the sparkles should make you blink
When I'm in her presence, I think I'm going to melt
Her heat is so intense; I can think of nothing else
We'll melt together into a ball
When I'm in her presence; I'm hers; she mine; we're all

Four Stages a Drink

A drink: a nibble, a dribble, a sip, or a drip
Four stages of life's predestined trip
Empty bottles, the drip bag three-fourth full
Fill my drip bag one-fourth vodka, then
turn me loose like a raging bull
One-fourth life, I'll nibble; two-fourth life, I'll dribble
Three-fourth life, I'll sip; four-fourth life, I'll refuse the drip
A drinking man is misunderstood
All drinkers aren't drunkards; that's good
If life deals a drinker a drunkard's hand
Clydesdales will haul his casket, amen
Me, I'll refuse the nonalcoholic drip
It's not predestined for my last trip
Empty bottles, bag three-fourth full
Add one-fourth vodka and ice till it's full

In a Garden

Life began in a garden; from there, it got real rough
Knowledge eaten from a tree; its fruit forbidden to tough

Me, me, I'm a sinner through and through
I've even eaten the fruit, and I've offered it to a few
In the beginning, every man spoke the same
tongue, his word each understood
He built a tower up to God; Babel struck him before he could

I've spoken to many women from many walks of life
It seems we all understand babble, struggle, and strife
My walk through life is not in vain
I walk to walk forbade to stand still to go insane
All my steps counted, my path measured just the same
God gave me life, and Jesus umps the game

Life began in a garden; there it did not end
I'm a sinner through and through; I will not pretend
The evil one walks the earth to and fro, looking for a friend

Kick the Can

Let's play Kick the Can; you know the one
Where we don't get old, we're having too much fun
Remember that game: Hide and Go Get It
I love you, baby girl, and I'm committed

Let's play that game called House
Let's get married, one each a spouse
Let's not forget the rings nor vows
Forsaking all others every day and right now

Let's play Two's Company and Three's a Crowd
Husband and wife, not too vain nor too proud
I'll lead the way; you help me steer
I'll be your hero; baby girl, have no fear

Let's rule this game called Life together
Our vows: it's we; it's us; it's forever
Our union will be so much fun
Let play Kick the Can; you know the one

My Summers and Winters

My early day's summer; my later day's winter
All through this weather, I've been a sinner
My summers were crawling with poisonous snakes
My winters are cold; my body shakes

Surviving the weather has been quite a work of art
Love is the fire that warms my cold, hardened heart
A four-letter word is not necessarily an action verb
If *love* were spelled *ball*, one could be thrown a strike or a curve

I've watched for love and hate in many eyes
I've read smiling faces trying to hide lies
I've felt more than one cold-blooded handshake
Fingers wrapped around mine like poisonous snakes

Love is the fire that warms this cold, hardened heart
Surviving the weather has been quite a work of art
My summers were crawling with poisonous snakes
My winters are cold; my body shakes

No One Else

You knew, didn't you
What was your first clue
I didn't need to tell you
Let's tell everyone; you want too

I think the world should know
But we don't have to put on a big show
It's all about us
We have to do what we must

No one else but us can make it
Work for us, so we must submit
We'll have to work hand in hand
It takes a woman and a man

The task at hand falls upon me and you
No one else is worthy for what we will do
You know what I'm saying is true
You knew; what was your first clue

Ocular

Eye one the spieling be
Eye one, ewe sea
Eye beeleaved eye could
Eye neu that eye wood
Eye one inn Tally has he
Inn nineteen hundread and ninty-three
Eye got every word write
Ewe wood have bin proud of me that nite
Spieling champion is who eye am
Axe me to speil any thang win ewe're in a jam
Ewe may knot beeleave
Butt soon ewe will conseed
Axe me and ewe'll sea
Why Eye one the spieling be

On My Way

As I travel, my way has been dim and light
Clustered with confusion, clarity, wrong, and right
Some days, I travel in uncontrollable fear
Fearing I'll never make my destination or come near

On my way, I've seen a lot
I've seen things I ought not
On my way, I've been greeted with dis and respect
Love, hate, envy, joy, hope, and regret

Yin and yang, darkness and light
Yin, she's gloom; yang, he's bright
On my way, yin and yang often fight
Dueling dualities—one's wrong; one's right

On my way, I've met you
It's obvious you've traveled with yin and yang too
Together we can make our own way as we
Plan our lives, our destiny

Peace of Mind

Now where is it
Where can it be found
How do I know it's missing
I'm lost when you're not around
Look at those watching
What do they see
You think they know about
About what's missing, what's troubling me
Watch their bewilderment; it's quite profound
Grasping for clues—is it square, or is it round
Could you have dropped it here on the ground
Don't worry: "It's always in the last place you look to be found"
When you're with me, I'm fine
I'm uplifted; I'm smitten; I'm floating on cloud nine
Your absence is cancer; your presence benign
Your love is peace of mind

See You around the Campfire

Yes, I'll see you around the heavenly campfire
We'll enjoy the spirit of the Lord, our hearts' desire
You've kindled a fire inside my heart
Even though we're worlds apart

The Lord has blessed us—yes, indeed
His love we share; that's all we need
Every knee shall bow; every soul shall confess
That Jesus is the Lord and through him we're blessed

I'll see you around the heavenly campfire
Our love, our faith, our prayers will ascend higher and higher
Yes, I'll see you around the heavenly campfire
We'll enjoy the spirit of the Lord, our hearts' desire

She's Waiting for Me

Goodbye, love; I'll be back; you hold it down
As my long walk began, I paused; I turned around
I stuttered, stepped into destiny, into beguile
I could see tears in her eye; she knew it'd be a while

Duty rang; I heard it call
I packed my bags; I'm prepared to give my all
I knew in the back of my mind; I knew...can't you see
She's waiting for me

Every day runs into the same
Every day, duty calls another name
I want to hold her in my arms one mo'gin
Our embrace will never end

I'll be back; we'll forever be hand in hand
Without her, I'm half a man
I knew; she knew...can't you see
She's waiting for me

Sweet Wine

Immature grapes make a bitter wine
Not weathered nor seasoned by time
I crave a mature, sweet wine
Sweetness derived from aging on the vine

Seasoned by time, aged by the sun, the wind, and the rain
Weathered, not beaten; full flavored, no distain
Aged to perfection over tried-and-tested years
Opened for my pleasure…this treasure; bottoms up…cheers

Wisdom bottled in a mature, sweet wine
Uncorked to reveal its bouquet so divine
Its essence seizes my lips and overpowers my tongue
Unmatched by the untried and the untested young

I crave a mature, sweet wine
Challenged by weather; seasoned by time
Full-bodied pleasure; its sweetness divine
Uncorked to reveal, its treasures are mine

Thanks

Thanks for sharing and giving
Life is precious and worth living
Thanks for your time
My days and nights are divine
Thanks for understanding my plight
Your love has shined a light

Your love has illuminated my way
Thank you for your encouraging words every day
Thank you for being you
And all that you do

Thanks for listening as I rant
Your patience is the love you grant

Thank you, I'll say it again
Thank you, my love, my friend
Thanks for giving
Thanks for your love, for sharing our living

The Man with Two Minds

Have you met him; you will in time
There lived a man with two minds
Unfortunately he was not duly smart
Both minds caused him troubles from the start

He wanted to be here when there
There was never the right where
He wanted to be taller and shorter than thee
He loved himself but if only he could be…

Stronger, faster, and better than before
Before what, he had almost everything and more
Simple questions caused him great pain
He read between the lines because he had been trained

To question the questioner before the question is asked
Never cared for speculations, only the facts
Listening for a message between every verb
Sitting dual minded, debating the meaning of every word

Their Options

A man stood over here
A woman stood over there
Their option: look at one another and stare
No one ever said life was fair

A man walked in the rain
A woman's tears were his pain
Their options: cooperate or suffer from the strain
No one ever said life was without loss or gain

A man asked what was wrong
A woman answered, "Are you strong?"
Their options: ask and answer the short of long
No one ever said life's conversations weren't prolonged

A man told a woman that he cares
A woman asked, "Are those bearer bonds or mutual shares?"
Their option: look at one another and stare
No one ever said life's cares were free of fare

What I Said

I said I'd call you every day
Life—it makes its own way
I promise I could not get through
The phone company was on strike…union dues

I said I'd get you a hundred Dove chocolate
ice cream bars; Doves, my love
I promise I was not trying to offend Dove ice
cream bars…you and me, still friends

I said I'd move heaven and earth for you
Get you a drink, tell you what I think, and buy you…too
I promised you heaven and earth; you heard, honeydew
I'll need some rest, then these things I'll do

I said I'd buy you what thing…
Hold on, did I hear my phone ring
I promise I'll call back soon
That's NASA; they want me on the moon

Missing You

I wish we were never parted
The separation had left me brokenhearted
Why did you have to leave
Was I the only one left to grieve

For years, I filled my life with others
They could not fill me; I felt smothered
Life without you was a trail of tears
Wounded, battered, and struggled for years

I wish I had never let you go away
I wished you back every day
I've wished for you to come on a sunbeam
Now, I know wishes come true just like dreams

You brought into my windows a ray of light
You brought sunshine into my life
Now we are one again
Missing you has come to an end

Encore

I like that backside you love to expose
I'd like to see it without any clothes
You've got to be tired of my lust
I'm not; I'd walk a hundred miles to get in
—them guts—

Close your eyes
Imagine me between those thighs
Think of the natural flow
Cream on top of cream as I blow

I'll imagine watching the top of your head
As I climb the wall behind the bed
No, no, no, don't stop
Like Folgers, it's good to the last drop

As we descend from on high but before we land
Encore, encore, the clapping of hands
I like that backside you love to expose
I'd like to see it without any clothes

Life's Clown

I've seen this person before today
On many occasions, I've heard him relay
Things I'd never venture to say
Even if I were playing nor would I in a verbal affray

But then again, I've often wished I could be him
I've heard their praises—yeah, them
They say he is as smart as a whip
He is wrapped tight; the world is in his grip

I've seen this person before today
When he is in my face, he has nothing spectacular to say
I've asked him who he thinks he is
As SMART as a whip; yeah, right—a real whiz

I've seen this person before today
Standing in my mirror with nothing to say
All in all, I love him being around
To him, life is a circus; and as for me, me, I'm life's clown

Cream Pie

I bet you thought I forgot about you
Our history is our story of the things we do
Do you remember how I'd get that look in my eyes
You knew I knew where you kept that cream pie

I bet you thought I forgot about us
Young in life's game, so eager for love and lust
Sunshine or rain, day or night
We knew one another; we knew from left to right

If I were a betting man, I'd float a large note
I'd bet on rooftops and in stairwells we sailed my sailboat
Wetter than the water between you and me
I'm the captain of the sailboat on your open seas

I bet you bet I forgot about you, my dear
Come closer; I'd like to whisper she love me nots in your ear
I love you; yes, I love you, and I got that look in my eyes
I knew you knew I knew where you keep the cream pie

Ask Him for Me

If you could ask him for me
I'll be here on bended knees
I've compiled a sin or two
It will take a while for him to review
A little item will you check
A small discretion, no, a major wreck
A check if you would—if you will, will you see if he will forgive
A sinner like me, allowed to live
A life so filled with more ups than downs
A life so blessed with more smiles than frowns
He's given to a person as unworthy as me
He's given to a person who's rarely on bended knees
I've been quick to cry for his intervention
I've been slow to obey or even mention
That I love the Lord because he heard my cry
Will you check; I don't mean to pry
Thanks for checking so discreetly
Checking if the Lord has forgiven me
He just touched my soul
My sins he's forgiven, those sins of old

Spending Time

I wrote this poem when I had nothing else to do
When I was reviewing my life, searching for a clue
As to the exact destination time flies to
When I'm having fun doing what I do

I wrote this poem when I was thinking about you
About the times we've spent thinking that maybe a clue
Maybe time doesn't fly because it's spent
That could explain where it went
Time is money, and money's on my mind
Excuse me, what has money to do with time
Nothing is more exclusively mine
Nothing is more precious to me than how I spend my time

I wrote this poem when I had time to spend
I realized that time doesn't fly, but it does come to an end
So today I'll be a big spender and spend
time with family and friends
PS Do me a solid; I'd like a little more time;
do you have any time to lend

My Baby

My baby, more or less, pound for pound
Your cries penetrate my ears as a sweet, sweet sound
Your tears hold my heart in agonizing suspense
Each teardrop melts my heart's defense

Words roll off my baby's tongue much too soon
Daylight turns into the luminous light of a full moon
Overnight the walking and talking have only just begun
My baby's investigating and debating serve for more than mere fun

From a microscopic seed, sprouted a mighty oak tree
My baby has risen in every degree
The shade I provide cannot be outgrown
As my baby ease into the light of a world unknown

With its treasures, its pleasures, its measures, and more
Have no fear, my baby; I'm your shelter; I'm your safe shore
My baby, my baby pound for pound
My baby, my baby, a sweet, sweet sound

Just as Cold

Enemy of my enemy is my friend
Cruel and inhumane justice has no end
Some cultures are centuries old
Justice for one and all is just as cold
From three-fourths a person to a whole
Still consider a boy no matter how old
Slashes opened and salted across backs
Being and not being could get you that
Today's justice fills pens; justice for just us has no end
For being and not being just us, it stretched necks
Stealing or not, it's justice, so what the heck
Centuries-old justice is very cruel
Is justice wheeled by just us the standard, or is it the rule
Teach me to hate those different from me
Teach me that justice will set me free
Centuries-old justice, all thieves lose their stealing hand
Is the adherence to this justice the cry for its disband
Enemy of my enemy is my friend
Cruel and inhumane, justice has no end
Centuries-old justice is afar
Cry for justice no matter where you are

With My Blindfold On

I woke every day, and I rested every night in the dark
I never knew of the light, the soul, the heart
My blindfold was my confidant, my companion, my friend
With my blindfold on, I navigated every crevice and bend

How was I to know; I was blinded to any fact
He said, she said, and they said that
He, she, and they proudly wore their blindfolds too
Them, all of them, informed me on what was false or true

The truth manifested itself from a book no longer unread
The words, their implications, ripped the blindfold off my head
My open eyes informed me that "he says,"
"she says," "they say" were dead

The letters created words which formed intelligence
I'm born again, illuminated, weighed, and measured in every sense
My light, my soul, my heart freed from ignorance
With blindfolds on, life is without reverence

A Special Day

What if everyone else could have a special day
Where lovers pretend to be bullfighters—
Ole matador's fight with swords made of sweets and tarts
Hey, they could pretend to slay their lover's heart

Give each other chocolate candy in boxes with diamond things
Old lovers and new lovers could perform in the bullrings
Olé, the crowd would affectionately cheer
As matadors slay lovers using words like "I love you, my dear"

What if everyone else could have a special day
Where lovers could run amok, frolic, and play
They could express their love from deep within their hearts
Hey, they could make romantic promises like "We'll never part"

If only there was a special day set aside
True lovers could be like us; lover would no longer be deprived
Our love is unrestricted, and it needs no special masquerade
I love you, and I wish everyone else could have a special day

Out of Step

Wet behind the ears, lack of respect
Knows everything about nothing and declares to reject
Some days I'm too hot, and other days I'm too cold
Youngblood rising swiftly; I'm outdated; I'm old

Youngblood created or restated, reblued, renewed it one mo'gin
Youth semiconscience to the world just before life ends
Running like a waterfall, overflowing banks and bounds
I'm "out of step"; you say why…am I
respected and lauded as renowned

Crawled, walked, ran, and I stood, sat, and lied
Study, learned, and taught before you were declared alive
Each man is a stepping-stone for followers on life's path
One added; one subtracted can another claim he invented math

"Out of step" is a misstatement; I'm the stepping-stone
Life's a collective, youngblood; you can't claim you done it alone
The milk souring on your breath has stained your upper lip
On the stepping-stone, life begins and ends; be careful not to trip

Step and Fetch

Ignorance, it champions that word like a first-place ribbon
Ancestors captured and cooped like award-winning pigeons
Herded to the market like cattle and murdered without regret
Discarded from Africa, then deprived of all self-respect
Ropes and chains adored their wrists and necks
Not one rope made of gold embroidered with diamond pecks
Their bounds were training tools used to teach the step and fetch
Whips licked and lapped the skin from
backs of our ancestral wretch
Past pains are forgotten by those who bore
no load nor felt the licks or laps
With first-place ribbons, they champion
degradation with laughter and backslaps
Three-fifth of a person, a perpetual child
stepped and fetched a heavy load
Too soon forgotten by first-place ribbon
holder who spit on those of old
Feel proud as the word rolls off your tongue, for many died for it
Degrade one another before the world; step and fetch, you can do it
Ignorance, it champions that word like a first-place ribbon
Our ancestors captured and cooped like award-winning pigeons

Today

Today, I'm too tired to think about
Facts and figures mixed with doubt
In my mind, I wish for just a little more
Order in the chaos from ship to shore
When it appears, everything will sort itself out
Bottom-pond water fishers catch deep-sea water trout
Usury at its best, lying when it says, "I love you"
Like a debt paid in full is a lie too, when interest is still due
Today, I'm too tired to dream about
A hot oil massage and a stream of cream from a spout
In my mind, I wished two times for my little piece
Not all of the pie, full in my eye, will give me my internal peace
When it appears, everything will work in my favor
Chocolate cake bites me with its bitter lemon flavor
A reminder to remember that, in life, there are only two guarantees
Today, life tastes like sugar; tomorrow,
sugar may taste like life's feces

As I Look

As I look, I wonder why
Am I not the sparkle in your eye
Why does a fire burn passionately
Why am I not the sailor and you my sea
As I look, I wonder why
Who allowed your star to fall from the sky
One touch, one kiss, one pronunciation, you saying my name
Is one more reason to love you without regret or shame
How can a fire breathe without a breeze
It should smolder and die, but it burns
my eyes and buckles my knees
Just one look and I smile
Just one look every once in a while
As I look, I wonder why
Why has so much time passed us by
Why does this fire burn in me
Why do I love you passionately

What I Hear

Every string has its length called until
Don't believe me? Just measure it if you will
Whether it's taunt or just dangling
It is what it is; it's just a string
Every song has its melody
Seeking its tone and tune in harmony
Its hook spoken and written in time
Its beat pulsates and vibrates each line
Every word is not the same
If it were, life would not be a game
Words soothe, smother, and choke
Words command, commit, and joke
Eyes can see more than ears can hear
Only few can see joy as terror in a tear
No matter the length, the song, the sight, the voice you're hearing
The message is always "Are you willing?"

I Have Only Eyes for You

No one else has planted love so deeply in my mind field
Feelings planted, your harvest has reaped a love so surreal
Our coupling fermented like wine, leaving us drunk in our musk
Moments measured in time are not lost moments between us
Winds swirl, stir, and blow, temperately carrying to me your scent
Honey fragrance stimulate my senses with your honey effervescence
Clouds cumulate in the sky; raindrops conceal drops I weep
Tears of wanting cumulate as I listen to raindrops in my sleep
Sunbeams dry drops to reveal love trails tracked across my face
In sunlight, I smile, knowing within you lies my amazing grace
Don't wonder about how it could have been, for we are today
Our time is patient, enduring, courageous,
and priceless in every way
No one has planted and reaped my love like you
No one has fermented the fruits of our love in honeydew
No one has survived the test of time; our perseverance is not taboo
No one else have caused me to go blind; I have only eyes for you

In Retrospect, I Reflect

In retrospect, I reflect an image for all to see
I can't see this image unless I look into a mirror of a reflection of me
My eyes, my windows, only outside myself; am I allowed to see
In retrospect, I do reflect a feeling I cannot see
When you peer in my windows, is there anyone
else, anyone else other than an image of me
Snake sends…an image
Kevin sends…a reflection
Neither sends everything, for they both are an image of me

In a Moment

When I greet a loved one, be it family or friends,
I do it with a hug, a kiss, or a hello
When I depart from my family or friends, I do the same as I go
I smile and I laugh as I enjoy life with one and the same
I'm also well aware that life is more than fun and games
In a moment, it comes like that
In a moment, life is given, and then it's snatched
Some succumb in their sleep
While other are escorted off the streets
In the heat of passion and like a flower, life blooms
In the heat of the moment, life is like a drama
scene taken in tragedy and gloom
Hold me, kiss me, and say I love you to me
if you only whisper it in my ear
I love you is all that I need if it's to be the
last thing in life I should hear
I love you one, and I love you all
I love you for nothing; I love you because you're big and you're small
I'm saying I love, and it's contagious; now you pass our love around
In our world, the sun will never go down

Untold

I never heard a word uttered; I never heard her name or story told
Her future on the brink of escalation, taken aback by a lost soul
Death in the streets, her body in piece, in peace in the cold
Her heartbeat forever taken, her attacker's display of a love so bold
I never heard a word uttered; I never heard her name or story told
Why did he say to her "I love you," then
deny her the right to grow old
Life is a balancing beam of ups and downs, rights and wrongs
Life was taken from a Nubian queen, leaving all of us less one strong
Her future on the brink of escalation, taken aback by a lost soul
A Nubian queen slain in the dawn of her life, her story still untold
Her body lay in peace; her spirit snatched by a rouge
She was a queen and a lady; she will never grow old

Within You

You can lean on me and others who are subject to tire
Motivational words and support are my attempts to inspire
If you really need help, it's the Lord you require
Success in what we do is fleeting, yet we all have desires
To build on what we have, to create our own empire
Let's all keep stepping forward and reaching for higher
Leave something behind for those bore and those sired
Not necessarily gold, diamonds, or sapphires
Self-love is the gift necessary in its entire
Love yourself; don't be some else's puppet on strings and wires
Don't lean too long; even the strongest of us will soon tire
Strength in yourself and belief in the Lord is required

Conspiracy

Conspiracy theories are rampant in a world devoid of light
Intellect succumbs to ignorance as the day succumbs to night
Questioning every answer, doubting deep within the heart
Wondering if it's a conspiracy, did Noah really build that ark
Inside a closed refrigerator, is the light on, or is it truly dark
Can a blaze burn a forest while a fire is lit from a single spark
Who left the cake out in the rain; I guess I'll never know
Secret recipes discussed in kitchens, Pillsbury's making all the dough
Is it a miracle that an open door could also be ajar
Language is a conspiracy on the intellect by far
What is said is not always what is meant
In a world devoid of light, breeds a conspiracy of ill intent

You're Forever

I love you in a special way
You're sweet like a Milky Way
You're a delicious treat at work, snack, or play
In my mind and heart, you're a welcome stowaway
In life, you may have too many
In death, there are not any
Only one remains till the end
Only one is more than a mere friend
Let's stay in touch with us
Ours is ours as such is such
More than a little but less than too much
You're forever, my love, my dream, my crush

Wrestling

I woke this morning with a smile on my face
Nights are a struggle, and days are grace
Every night, I fight the good fight
Each morning, I wake to greet the daylight
I am still the king of my wrestling ring
Poised at length, awaiting the pleasures a night may bring
Famed for my dip and jab followed by my hip block
The only countermove for it is the famed leg lock
Some days I refuse rest or sleep
I greet the daybreak without feeling weak
Tossing and turning, vacillating in and out
Eyes open, then closed, I'm fighting the good fight, no doubt
Weather tempered hot or cold, whether rain or shine
Struggle whether you're young or old; a
little strain will clear your mind
I woke this morning with a smile on my face
Nights are a struggle, and days are grace

One for One

Let us take a moment and pause here
To make a fact evidently clear
If you fail to listen, then you fail to hear
Assume nothing while you draw near
Two were and one told the tale
Twelve convicted and one judge to hell
"Am I my brother's keeper?" he said
Whose turn was it to watch him; I did know he was dead
One had two, and one had none
Now one of the ones possessed the gun
The possessed gun expelled a bullet, which made none two
The possessed never learned to fish, so one does what one do
Let us take a moment and pause here
To make a fact evidently clear
You are your brother's keeper and shepherd one, if you will
Teach one how to fish before another one learns to kill

Eye Cried

Eye cried today
Eye cried, and Tongue had nothing to say
Eye sniffed the tears, and Nose turned the other way
That sun dried that rain, but it denied Eye a single ray
Eye must say first
Eye am dying it red at first thirst
Eye cried a bucket of tears
Not one word did Her Ears hear
Her Ears, they must have been strained
Eye knew, and Her Ears heard Tongue was trained
To tell the tales of love spoken softly and often heard
Eyes and Ears wide open and not a sound or a word
Eye left the windows wide open to my soul
Tongue must have caught a cold
Eye blinked maybe once or twice
Eye knew Tongue had issues; he nothing nice
Tongue failed to tell you "I love you" every second of the day
Eye cried today because Tongue he did betray

Failure's Defeat

Don't give in to Failure's why
Each attempt, each effort, each try
Failure infects the state of mind
I am; I can; I will be fine
Let Perseverance's light break into anew
Exhume self-confidence, and do all you can do
Should Life's rain pour, please don't drown
Head faced up forward and never face down
Failure is like a raging bull in a china glass shop
Smashing expensive dreams and halting hopes full stop
Failure, with its many flaws, is truly weak
Self-defeating thoughts are its strength
and a victim of Failure's defeat
Don't give in to Failure's why
Perseverance trumps Failure; always try
Weighed and measured in kind
I am; I can; I will be fine

I Can Explain

How can I explain
To begin with, they appeared the same
Everything that glitters is not gold
At first glance, even you would have been sold

After all has been said
What appeared gold was red
Really you had to be there
Me, me, I pulled out my hair

Here is how it happened to me
No, no, I don't need glasses to see
It's unbelievable till this very day
Don't shake your head; don't say no way

Listen because I believe; I can explain
Even though they appeared to look the same
Remember, everything that glitters is not gold
At first glance, even you might have even been sold

This Tree

I watched this tree grow old
Or maybe this tree watched me
In summer's heat and winter's cold
It stood majestically
Who would have known
Now that we're both grown
How far its shadow would reach
Shelter and stability, a survivor's lesson, do teach
Time ages the strong and lulls the weak to sleep
Time grew this tree which vowed it will never leave
During relentless storms, it stood fast without a single peep
Leaves and branches fell, but the truck and roots never grieve
This tree taught without lecture; now its lessons I do teach
My shadow has grown, and time has expanded my reach
I watched this tree grow old
Or maybe this tree watched me

Watching TV

I recall playing in the sand
Playing an air guitar in my imaginary band
Worrying how long I would get to watch TV
Nine o'clock never escaped me

I recall waking from a self-imposed sleep
Realizing society expected me to sow so I can reap
No more lunch boxes or brown bags from
under a roof I fondly knew as home
I had to build it, lease it, rent it, or buy a roof known as my own

I recall saying for the first time, "Don't
tell me what to do. I'm grown"
Proclaiming, "I will do what I want, when
I want," and often I was wrong
I recall managing funds, fun, and then some just to find
Chaos and confusion had called shotgun or front seat on my time

Peace of mind, love for life, and respect
for others are my late-life show
Believe these words: "You reap what you sow"
Under my roof, my seeds worry how long they can watch TV
Nine o'clock never escaped me

Word Game

Words that are spelled or that sound alike confuse this brain
I mint money; I meant to explain
Read only the red here and hear only what is read
Write only the rite of passage on the right side of my head

A mite might have understood this word game
Wind blows, and you wind rope; when is a win the same
Sight the site, and I will cite just a few words
At night, a knight heard; two or more cows is a herd

From on high, she waved hi over there; you see the sea
Too many times, two people are needed to agree
Which eye did I see that witch eat a fly, then fly two for one
A mayor rode a mare, but no one elected won

Sore arms threw, and birds soar through
While in the wild, do be careful not to step in dew due
Words must be used, but which one to use is hard to explain
Words that are spelled or that sound alike confuse this brain

Rated

My thoughts are subject to being weighed and measured
By a committee made up of whoever
Would take the time for such an endeavor
In hindsight, it's not so bad
Being weighed and measured, I'm glad
To be on the minds of those like you
Who would attempt to decipher a meaning from no clue
About what goes on in a place that can't be spanned
My thoughts and emotional experiences untouched by hands

Whoever…have you ever thought to think
Sneezed to blink
Pondered to wonder why
One would stick a needle in your eye
Digress with me as we egress
Through a place that is more than a mess
Between thoughts, between lines are rhymes
Without weight, length, or height; but there
are bells, and there are chimes

I Breathe

She means more than fresh air; she's more than a simple breeze
She's my lungs; as she inhales and she exhales, I breathe
Her warmth heats my passion, and I ignite the sun
Melting icebergs in boiling oceans and
melting candle wax, watch it run
Under heavy cloud covers, come the wet and the rain
Splashing and dripping…she's calling my name
Does the sun ever set; does the moon ever rise
I have not taken notice; she has engulfed my eyes
Love is like the air; it can't be seen
It can be felt but not touched like an X-rated dream
Hearts racing, bodies trembling, a hot shower and mirrors steamed
She is my hot cup of coffee with extra sugar and more cream
Life isn't always as life cares to seem
Passion and love are not illusions; time lost
without them cannot be redeemed
She means more than fresh air; she's more than a simple breeze
She is my lungs; as she inhales and she exhales, I breathe

Secret Place

In a secret place, higher than any shelf
There is love; I put it there myself
This love is aged and very refined
You can take it all at once or a little at a time

In an undisclosed location, in a place unsaid
Passionate thoughts flicker like candles burning hot and red
Passion and candles alike will never burn cold
Never blow out the fire and never let passion grow old

When the stars are all aligned
We will be as one, so watch for the sign
Passion and *compassion* are the watchwords for today
One without the other is like *fore* without *play*

In a secret place, higher than any shelf
There is love; I can't keep it all to myself
Flickering thoughts of us are burning uncontrollably in my head
You and me, in an undisclosed location, in a place unsaid

Don't Worry 'Bout

Don't worry 'bout me straying or looking to see
In my heart and soul, you're deeply rooted, rooted vividly
Our path has one direction, and on this path, there's only we
Straying off our path is unconsidered; the view is for all to see
Don't worry 'bout us or where you think we stand
In my heart and soul, you're famous, and I'm your biggest fan
I remember your first appearance with its spectacular reviews
I was dazed; I was stunned to be the one that you would choose
Don't worry 'bout your hair turning gray and your age turning old
In my heart and soul, your hair is perfect,
and your age is worth gold
Memories are a reflection of our life together
and our feelings truly felt
Time is ours to play with; it's the hand that we were dealt
Don't worry 'bout whether I'll love you forever and a day
In my heart and soul, you're loved in ways words cannot convey
I can't express in words what loving you means to me
I'll capsulate by saying it's deeper than deep could be

Entropy

Can you believe the status report on our society
Reportedly, it's the most advanced practicing the dogma entropy
Review your reviewer every now and again
Between wars and global warming, did your team win

My summation on what has happened in the past
Our society on a sinking ship, and it's sinking fast
Me…me, I think I'm suffering from a mental defect
No matter how bad it is, it's okay; it's cause and effect

'Cause one had a dream, vision, and mission to get ahead
One dreamless plotter plotted to leave one dead
One believed the chicken came before the
egg; one believed; one was misled
One cast the first stone, and millions suffered
while countless others bled

Forecasting is a glimpse into the future while reflecting on the past
Entropy is the forecast, and our society
is sinking, and it's sinking fast
Can you believe the status reported on our society
Reportedly, it's the most advanced in the doctrine of entropy

What I Think

What I think, it has been asked at last
I think my thoughts are all thoughts of the past
I think two can do more if three were one less
I think a man without an opinion should wear a dress

I think if a bullfrog had a glass… I'll say rump
I think it would crawl on its belly; it definitely wouldn't jump
I think you thought you knew more than a lot
I think more than should be less than why or why not

I think in a year that I'm not yet ready to announce
I think tons of this or that will be measured by the ounce
I think we all drink three to eight glasses of raw sewage
I think, if fish could walk on land, that's where it might do it

What I think, I'm glad it has finally been asked
I think, if it were not for the other hole,
one's mouth would also be one's as
I was saying about my thoughts and the past
I think; I thought that I was glad you asked

I Hate Nothing

Tolerance should help uproot or alleviate
Intolerance deeply rooted in one's heart as hate
Me, me, I hate everything about nothing as of late
I hate nothing about everything; therein lies the debate
Tolerating everything if nothing is on the plate
Nothing has troubled me for so long it's too hard to contemplate
Tolerating the void, nothing dares to create
Everything is nothing if nothing is allowed to procreate
Intolerance of others' thoughts, ideas, or pigmentation, I can't relate
Intolerance of others for nothing culls my hate
Intolerant of everything is truly nothing great
When everything is intolerable, hate and nothing else can dominate
Me, me, I hate everything about nothing as of late
I hate nothing about everything; therein lies the debate
When the tables set before you and intolerance is on the plate
Everything can be tolerated, but nothing set before can be ate

Fun and Games

Step right up; "everyone a winner" is what life touts as its decree
Fun and games is what life offers at different levels of degree
Life within life, there's a sublevel called fun and games
We laugh with or we laugh at, not all laughter is the same
Bench setting, if preferred, but is unheard
of as life's intent or notion
Either you're in or you're out; don't fake in life
or move through it in slow motion
Are you here for the fun, or are you here for the games
Barefoot and naked is how we entered; we'll exit loved or shamed
Step right up; everyone is a winner
Step to life's table, and guess what's for dinner
A wise man said not everyone seated would necessarily eat
It's all fun and games until the hungry are fed laughter at the feast
Don't let push come to shove; don't let
laugher ruin the fun and games
We laugh with or we laugh at, not all laughter is the same
Step right up; everyone is a winner in life's fun and games
Barefoot and naked is how we entered,
and we'll exit loved or shamed

My Heart

Coming to a theater near you, come one and all
Come see MY HEART on stage, in her hands this fall
MY HEART, I pulled it from my chest for my Amazonian queen
My eyes were wide open, but my mind believes she's a dream
She'll never have to ask; I've already gave
I'm not fighting to escape; MY HEART is her slave
Bound not by ropes or a single thread
Held steadfast by her presence and without a word said
Her inner and outer beauty exude from her sweet zest for life
MY HEART's delight or plight…my captor surrenders to be a wife
MY HEART skips a beat as it runs wild, just to see her smile
In my arms is where she belongs, if just for a little while
MY HEART's onstage listening to hear her calling my name
She's MY HEART's audience of one, the one MY HEART will entertain
Coming to a theater near you, come one and all
Come see MY HEART on stage, in her hands this fall

One Word

If I had only one word left to convey
I'd take my time not to waste that word away
In the proper setting and on an appropriate day
I'd rehearse the word within, and then I'd say
In one word, I'd tell you my thoughts
In one word, I'd tell you we ought
In one word, I'd tell you an awful lot
In one word, I'd tell you the whys of why nots
That one word would burn within your heart and brain
That one word I would do my very best to explain
That one word could change our whole life
That one word could change all our struggles and strife
If I had only one word left to convey
I'd tell you and you only on that special day
I'd hold your hands in mine; I'd look into your eyes
Love would be that one word shared between you and I

Questions

Why does one do this or that for another
Why does it take two to flock like birds of a feather
Why does life crawl, walk, and run into itself
Why do I want you for myself

How many days are in a new year
How many drops can one eye tear
How can joy come from pain
How can love cause a heart to beat again

Is magic more of a trick than an illusion
Is wanting you more of a dream littered with confusion
Is there enough time for us in a day
Is one moment just one more second away

What must I do to have you more
What separates a relationship from shore
What can I do...no...no, what can I say
What if I told you I'll love you forever and one day

Be My World

Come to me, love; come be my baby girl
I've chosen you carefully to come be my world
Everything I do for you is without compromise
Let me be that twinkling star that twinkles in your eyes
Be my world; one is truly lonely without two
Be my world, and I will revolve my life around you
Be my baby girl, and I will be yours for true
No one will dampen our love as mornings are damped by dew
Wrap your arms around me every time we greet
We'll close our eyes, then press our lips every time we meet
In your hands, I've placed within it a very valuable key
Use it to open my loving heart, a heart filled with glee
Come to me, love; come be my baby girl
Open my heart; you have the key; come be my world
Be my world, and I will revolve my life around you
Be my world; one is truly lonely without two

Have I Told You

Have I told you lately how I feel
My feelings about you are for real
You're the reason life is worth living
To share a love with another is like Thanksgiving

Thank you for the time you spend with me
Thank you for your presence, allowing me to see
Thank you for your hugs and kisses shared as we
Thank you for giving me a sweet taste of thee

I feel there's not enough time for us to play
Days turn into night; so quickly it's yesterday
Another day behind and the future coming soon
Let's take our feeling higher; let's shoot for the moon

Have I told you I love you more as our time slips away
Have I told you, within my heart, you are forever and a day
Have I told you my heart pumps blood just for you
Today, I'm telling you my feelings: I love you

I Slept

Baby girl, how did you sleep
I slept well, and I very deep
In my dream, I had quite a spectacular view
I saw roses, chocolate candy, and sweet honeydew

As I moved a little closer to the king-size bed
I saw your beautiful long, slender legs
Not to mention those creamy, luscious thighs
I could hardly believe your beauty exposed before my eyes

Your perfectly formed soft breast met me as we kissed
Our passion burned; our sweat streamed into a foggy mist
We melted into one another like hot melting wax
Our temperatures kept rising until we reach our climax

We held each other like Siamese twins
As our passion rekindled, we climaxed again
Baby girl, how did you sleep
I slept well, and I slept deep

Stop, Call Me

Stop, don't move; you see watch I saw
Don't disturb her; it's probably against the law
Do you think she's from here or from another world
Call me Captain Kirk; I'm going to make her my girl

Stop, listen closely; I think I hear her saying my name
Do you think she knows I'm a hunter of beautiful game
Do you think she'll let me capture her between red satin sheets
Call me the hurter; look at that beauty; I'll sweep her off her feet

Stop, did you see that? Did you see her looking this way
Do you think she knows? Do you think she knows the play
Do you think her game's tight? Is she ready for me tonight
Call me good night; I'll step to her right; I've trained for her delight

Stop, I think she's…no…wait…yes, she's coming near
Do you think I should make eye contact or circle 'round to her rear
Stop, don't move; you do see watch I saw
Don't disturb her; it's probably against the law

We've Discovered
Our Love in You

We've wanted, but we've yet to find a love so true
We've searched the world over looking for love in every who
We never imaged finding love sought in you
Days in, days out—me, myself, and I have
sought love in one of four, not two
I've talked to me about why myself feels the way I do
I can't answer or explain to myself, nor can me explain to you
We only know that, without you, our days
and nights are misty and blue
Me, myself, and I agree love equals one, not four or two
We've paced and pondered not only to but fro
We've walked in, then out of a series of
open, then closed doors and mo'
In every who, I've asked myself, Is this the love I've sought for me
In every who, the answer was no, but now we agree
We've wanted a love, but it's never been for true
We sought our love in every who, but now we agree
We've discovered our love in you
Me, myself, and I agree that we and you equal one, not four or two
We've wanted, and now we've found our love so true

Some Days

When I wake in the morning, I pray
I pray this will be our wonderful someday
A day that brings me closer in time to you
Our thoughts, expectations, desires, and coitus too
We are like flowing water, yet water drops apart
Our love storms and floods the banks of our hearts
Our path is darkened with issues as we travel
through a Sherwood-like forest called life
Like Robert Frost, we've chosen the path less traveled by,
and that's made all the difference in struggle and strife
On those days, when we are out of sync
I pray for our wonderful someday, and I think
Life is one day in and one day out
Our wonderful somedays are what life's about
Some days are great while other days lack
Some days are wonderful, and they're always welcomed back
When I wake in the morning, I pray
I pray this will be another wonderful someday

Candy Store

Can I have some candy; aren't you a candy store
I want something sweet, and it's you I'm craving for
I want a bit o' honey from your soft marshmallow lips
I want that juicy fruit dripping from
between those cotton-candy hips
I want all your sweetness captured by my caramel eyes
I want that cream-filled Suzy Q between those creamy thighs
Your honey buns are what I've been looking at
I want them later on as a midnight snack
The Cookie Monster maybe a ravenous beast
I'll shut Sesame Street down if you're my feast
I'm having Skittles, Starburst, rainbow candy dreams
Mouth-watering flavors and frosty liquid cream
The very thought of you makes me want you more
Your cinnamon and spicy heart is what I adore
Can I have some candy; aren't you're a candy store
I want something sweet, and it's you I'm craving for

Should I Tell Her

Should I tell her that I love her, or is that a mistake
My heart says yes, and my mind says wait
Love is another one of those four-letter words
Spoken out of turn, it's rude, and it's not even heard

Should I tell her she has captured my mind, the whole of me
This is straight talk on the level, 180, not 360, degrees
Am I the one, or am I only one
It doesn't matter as long as we have our fun

Should I tell her my heart bleeds for her amazing grace
I want her presence always and her loving embrace
Am I driving recklessly in love? Should I stay in my lane
Is being first in her heart too much for only one to gain

Should I tell her once or twice a day
Should I tell her at work, after a snack, or during our play
Should I tell her that she is the one sent to me from above
I should tell her every day; boo, it is you that I love

A Little Crazy

I'm just a little crazy 'bout you, my doctor said
He's going to loosen the straps on my bed
Tomorrow, he said he might let me out
All I have to do is deal with my doubts

I doubt if he knows why I've fallen
I've told him I hear your voice calling
I hear you even when you're not here
I feel your presence when you're not near

I see you in my sleep descending from above
A heavenly body carried on the wings of doves
You've touched my heart, and I'll never be the same
They strapped me to this bed; you'd think I'm insane

I'm just a little crazy 'bout you, my doctor said
He's going to loosen the straps on my bed
I think of you constantly, and I love you without any doubt
Tomorrow, I think my doctor might let me out

Finite

Our hearts have a finite number; they pump and beat
Let's spend that time together between silk sheets
Let's smile and laugh about the present and the past
Let's live like those pumps and beats are our last
Our time together is numbered, so let's both be sweet
Like children in a candy store, let's indulge in our treats
Let's dance to the musical pumps and beats of our heart
Let's constantly make love passionately; let's never be apart
Our time together is measured like ticks and tocks
We're bound together in time like hands on a clock
My time is dedicated to you; use it up however you chose
We must use our time together wisely, or we both lose
Our hearts have a finite number; they pump and beat
Let's spend our time together between silk sheets
Let's hug and kiss like life has no end
Let's always be true lovers and friend

Really for True

You're really for true; you're the woman of my dreams.
I've kissed you from head to toe; I've tasted your candy and cream.
I want you to know, without a doubt, I'm yours; and that's for true.
I've smiled and laughed with many faces but none as lovely as you.
You're unaware of how you make me feel inside and out.
Joy and happiness are ambiguous words; they leave room for doubt.

Love is a very strong word, and it varies in meaning and in degree.
Love is the only word that expresses how I feel, and I use it sparingly.
I think of you from time to time each second,
each minute, and each hour.
If I were a bumblebee collecting pollen,
you would be my only flower.

I see you in my sleep; I feel your presence when you're not around.
Image we are lovebirds nesting on a cloud;
our love is heaven bound.
Some days, I want nothing more than to
hear your voice and see your face.
My feelings are lost in words, which can't
express my thoughts of grace.
I've kissed you from head to toe; I've tasted your candy and cream.
You're really for true; you're the woman of my dreams.

Straight Facts

I've tap danced on the head of a safety pin
I've drank milk and turned it into gin
I've skipped through fires wearing gasoline draws
I've backhanded a polar bear and took its teeth and claws

I'm not bragging about all that I can do
I'm spitting straight facts; you caught a clue
I'm not the tallest, but I'm the strongest by far
I'm known to stop traffic with one hand and hold hundreds of cars

I could change the time with a thought from day to night
I could, with one word, change every wrong to a right
I could jump over Mount Everest and land on the moon
I could run around the world twice before this afternoon

Out of all these things, there's only one thing I can't do
I can't quench my insatiable thirst for you
I want you more than a fish needs water to breathe
I love you more than my straight facts are to believe

Ab Ovo

Every fairy tale has an ending; that's very clear
How a fairy tale starts is always in myths and fear
Looking back in the past without a magic hourglass
His story and her story, different as time does pass
Her story may have started on a starlit night in June
His story may have started under the light of a full moon
They may not remember the meeting exactly the same way
Neither would believe that they really met during the day
They knew it all began; the question is why it had to end
A Latin's quote: *ab ovo* means from the egg is where it began
Ab ovo, they were fairy-tale lovers before they were true friends
After coitus, they never cuddled, shared, or held hands
Ab ovo is where the fairy tale fell apart
Ab ovo, sex came before the giving of hearts
From the beginning is where the tale ended, it seems
From the beginning, their fairy tale started
at the end of a bad dream

You Move Me

I need to talk, and I need to talk to you
I've held my tongue until my face turned blue
I felt it in my mind about a thousand times
I've had it inscribed into braille for the blind

I've had it videotaped so others could read my lips
I've held it so tightly, clinched like a pair of vice grips
I've done some things, and I'm willing to do more
I've talked the talk; I've walked the walk from ship to shore

Not only have I said how much I love you in my heart
My love is like the Rock of Gibraltar, a nature's work of art
I have one thing to tell you, and it's unheard of but must be said
When the sun rises and sets, you rise and set in my head

You move me like the wind moves a sailing ship
You move me through the ups and downs of our relationship
You move me in ways no other could successfully do
You move me deep within beyond the words I love you

As the World Turns

As the world turns and we search for tomorrow
Let's share pleasant memories without regret or sorrow
Let's rise like the sun to brighten each other's day
Our lives, like clear skies, will never be cloudy or gray

Our memories are our mirrors reflecting thoughts of yesterday
Let's create memories that shine like the sun's brightest rays
Let's shine our light all night and all through the day
Let's never have a dark memory or a bad word to say

Our rainbow passion will be seen before and after every kiss
At the end of the rainbow, love is our treasured bliss
As the world turns, place your hand in mine to hold
As we search for tomorrow, we'll grow old but not cold

Each moment, let's create bright memories of our past
Each day, let's live as if each day were our last
Let's share pleasant memories without regret or sorrow
As the world turns and we search for tomorrow

R U 4

It's half past the time it was before
One eye watching the clock and the other the door
The cell phone is textless; it will not do its thing
Where is the message…why doesn't it ring

A carrier pigeon flew out the other day
No carrier pigeon returned, no message per se
A runner was sent to deliver the word
No runner returned, no word heard

A search party has been quickly dispatched
Looking for an SOS, where's it at
Could that be the message, or is that a clue
No message returned, no postage due

The message sent was "R U 4 me"
No message returned; O, now I C
It's half past the time it was before
One eye watching the clock and the other the door

Superhero

Being a superhero isn't all it's cracked up to be
Saving the same woman from life's travesties
Fighting villains who do nothing but playa hate
There are two superheroes with whom I can relate
Superman loved and had Lois Joanne Lane by his side
His true face unseen by the world; he thought had to hide
At the Daily Planet, as a news reporter,
Clark Kent hid from his alter ego
For the love of one woman, he was willing lose it all to let her know
Spider-Man loved a few, but he had Mary
Jane Watson on his main line
He weaved a wicked web as he hid from
the world and captured her mind
At the Daily Bugle, as a news photographer, Peter
Parker hid from his alternate identity
For the love of MJ, he was willing to give up
his web-slinging ways for eternity
Superman and Spider-Man are two superheroes hiding for all to see
They were willing to sacrifice themselves for the love of their ladies
Spider-Man put away his mask; Superman gave
up his cape; both did it for love's sake
They put them down, then picked them
because love is a give-and-take

I Want to Believe

Blinded by love is hard to conceive
With my eyes wide open, I can't perceive
My world spinning out of control
In the middle of winter, I'm standing outside naked, out in the cold

Through rainy windows, I only see the clear blue sky
I walk out in the rain so no one can see me cry
My world is crumbling, and my rose garden is about to die
I tell myself it's okay, but I can't even tell the truth from a lie

Naysayer tell me I'm being deceived
I don't want to hear that: I want to believe
My lover loves me as us and as we
My lover loves me unconditionally

All I can say to the naysayer is I want to believe
I love my lover, and my lover would never deceive
Blinded by love, I could never conceive
My lover loves me; I want to believe

Honeybee, My Flower

You told me you were forever mine
Your springs and summers were our time
I saw what I saw, but I did not see
You were not the flower blossoming for me

You were just biding your wintertime
You never wanted just me anytime
You made promises with your rose petals crossed
You told me I could have your pollen before first frost

I knew in my heart you were only for me; we were happy
You were my blossoming flower, and I was your honeybee
You promised you'd only blossom for me, so why did you lie
I saw you blossom for a hummingbird and a butterfly

Now, I have to look for a new blossoming bud
A blossoming flower that will only show me love
You told me you were forever mine
How could I have been so blind

There Can Be No Us without U

There can be no us without u
Let's be as one; it's not as lonely as being two
There can be no we without e
Let's come together, you and me

Life is so lonely when there's only I
Alone in thought, a tear-filled eye
I is the loneliest a person could ever b
It's like being stranded on an island in the middle of the c

Hold me, and I'll hold you true
Love me as much as I love you
Look into my eyes, the windows to my soul
In them are feelings no words have told

Without you, I'm like a puzzle missing all my parts
Without you, words could never come from my heart
There can be no us without u
Let's be as one; it's not as lonely as being two

Your Presence Is My Gift

Money can buy many things
Rubies, pearls, and diamond rings
Houses, cars, and airplanes too
Islands and yachts, just to name a few

I've heard it said that money couldn't buy love
It buys red roses and twelve white doves
I've heard it said money is at the root of all evil
Dressed up like royalty, aired and regal

My gift not even Bill Gates could buy
Only you can afford it and have the right to deny
Your presence is my gift, and it's the gift of a lifetime
Your presence is precious and heavenly divine

Money can buy many things
It's even been known to fulfill many dreams
Your presence is my gift shared between you and I
Your presence is my gift; I'll treasure it till I die

My Love Is Alive

Thirst, hunger, and the need to breathe
Love's three ingredients mixed with a need to believe
I believe in love's passion and compassion
My love is alive, and it needs constant attention

My love is thirsty for a tall drink of sweetness
Hot, steamy, and creamy are my love's weakness
I'm dehydrated, thirsty, and dripping, soaked and wet
My love is quenched by her presence, her touch, and her sex

My love is hungry for a tasty, sweet feast
Hungrier than a starving, a raging, a ravenous beast
My love needs to be fed; that's all that needs to be said
Love's passion and compassion feed my hunger and fill my head

My love breathes; yes, a breath keeps my fire burning hot
Without a breath of fresh air, I'd suffocate, would I not
Inhales and exhales fan my fire's passionate flames in love
I believe love quenches my thirst, feeds my
hunger, and allows me to breathe

Will You Ever

Will you ever feel the same way I do
My heart cries "I love you" with every thought of you
My words poorly explain my thoughts and my views
My words are to let you know it's you that I chose

Will you ever see me as I see you
Flawed yet flawless, perfect for me—yes, yes, you
I see you in my life if just for a moment or two
In those moments, I will show you it is for you I will do

Will we ever be as peanut butter is to jelly and to jam
A coupling so delicious it's like you and me being one, I am
One plus one is two; you plus me is we; do the math, and you'll see
Our lives add up; we are meant for one another; we are meant to be

Will you ever love me the same way I love you
My heart cries "I love you" every second or two
Don't take my love for granted; it's all I have to give
My love is alive, and it's for you my love lives

The Weeping Willow Wept

The weeping willow wept; the mighty oak grieves
Fall came too soon, and they both had to shed their leaves
They stood rooted by the river, shedding leaves into its flows
Watching the river meander while being caressed as the wind blows

They knew the fall was coming, and the winter would drop in
They also knew a life without seasons means a life due to end
Each leaf that dropped into the river splashed without a sound
The only leaves heard were those rustling on the ground

The weeping willow wept because the mighty oak would leave
Life without the mighty oak would be unbearable indeed
Willow cried all night into the middle of the eve
Stood there slumped over in a somber plea

The mighty oak grieves for the weeping willow's plight
Willow lost all its leaves and wept all night
Lean on me when all your leaves are gone
Oak assured willow that it would never be alone

Push or Pull

My love is hungry, so I ate; now I can never get full
One end of the rope says push; the other end says pull
I held my breath an hour inside a vacuum sweeper
Little Miss Muffet meets me there; BOY! She is a keeper

I fell in love, but love was emptier than air
My heart broke in the fall, and I'm without a spare
I drank from an empty glass; my thirst plenty quenched
I slept in a dry lakebed; I woke up very drenched

Yesterday, we talked, and last night we never spoke
I lay awake, so this morning, I never woke
The alarm sat to ring, but it stood up and never rang
The orchestra played lovely, but the soloist never sang

With my eyes wide open, I can see clearly into the dark
The warning signs read "Gas Line Broken,"
but what's life without a spark
My love is hungry, so I ate; now I can never get full
One end of the rope says push; the other end says pull

Win or Lose

Win or lose, I'm in the game
In life and in love, the odds are all the same
Look me in the eyes and see what you will
I'm playing this game for keeps and the sure thrill

Fade me, if you will, when I'm holding the dice
Seven or eleven, I win, and you may lose twice
Come correct and think about it before you enter my joint
I'm in it to win it, so when I'm rolling, I'm always on point

If I should hit snake eyes out the box and now it's your roll
Don't feel sorry for me; it's been real and as good as gold
I may or may not always play this game by the rules
Never forget your point because, in life and in love, I can be cruel

Win or lose, I'm in this game
If I should ever lose, there will be no shame
In life and in love, I'm rolling these dice to win
Seven or eleven, life or love, fade me one mo'gin

Board Game Love

Let's take a long, loving ride on the Exotic Reading Railroad train
Ride the main line to ecstasy, passing romance,
then back down memory lane
I'll buy up Boardwalk, and we'll live in a penthouse suite
Make love all through the day to the rhythm of our heartbeats
Candlelight dinner, rose petals, and a soothing whirlpool
Hot oil massage, king-size bed, and me, love's biggest fool
Giving you all that I have to offer from my head to my feet
On a platinum platter, my love is served, and my heart is your treat
I love you 360 degrees; that's not a mystery
The real who done it is why Ms. Scarlet with
a pipe in the library on ecstasy
Most people go through life searching for
and never finding a lover's clue
Case closed, it me loving you in the parlor and in the bedroom too
The Parker Brothers, unlike me, claim to have a monopoly
They don't have a clue about loving you; it's an unsolved mystery
Let's take a long, loving ride on the Exotic Reading Railroad train
Ride the main line to ecstasy, passing romance,
then back down memory lane

When I Step

When I step, you step; don't lag behind
I'm about my paper when I on the grind
I'm about that woman when that woman about me
If she got my bread spread, I got her cheese

When I step, you step, and you step very high
Step up or step out, I'm in this game till the day I die
If you don't know the rules, the game will play you
See no evil, hear no evil, speak no evil, and pay your dues

When I step, you step up to the plate
Don't hesitate; don't even let it be said too late
Tricks are for kids; don't be like that silly rabbit
Bugs may be funny; I'm not Elmer; I'll let you have it

When I step, you step; I'm in this game for life
Uphill, downhill, good times in struggles and strife
When I step, you step; don't lag behind
I'm about my paper when I on the grind

Whasa Name

Will whasa name be there for you
Does whasa name even have clue
When did whasa name audition for the part
Has whasa name been down from the start

Our hands are dirty; we're putting in work just to live
Whasa name must be washing dishes with Palmolive
After the fireworks and last firecracker bounces off the street
I bet whasa name has a cold skeet skeet

Don't let whasa name dig a hole in your head
We're dug in dirty; whasa name looking for a dirty bed
Never get to close to whasa name and fall asleep
Whasa name in the cut, looking down at you six feet deep

You may think you don't know who I'm talking about
You know whasa name, and you have your doubts
Ask yourself, Has whasa name paid dues
Will whasa name be there for you

Even Though You Were Not There

Even though you were not there
We made love all night without a care
I slept with you on my mind, and little else I
wore your favorite birthday suit—myself

I smelled your sweetness, the aroma you wear
We embraced each other as if we were braided hair
We must have tossed and turned all night
Sweaty and exhausted, what a pleasant delight

I woke this morning, and you had mysteriously vanished
Our passion last night: daylight quickly banished
My mind played a cruel game with my heart
It said we were together and we would never be apart

Even though you were not there
We can reminisce about last night; let's clear the air
Tell me why you only come to me in my dreams
Why our love is just a fantasy, why is nothing as it seems

Air

You believe that silly saying: you are what you eat
I got a heart of gold; I'm a product of these streets
I've got that Midas touch, so I've been told
Everything that I touch is sure to turn to gold

I got a lot of love flowing through these veins
Nasties have attempted bloodlettings; all were in vain
Playa haters, beware; I go live, and I go big in this game
You know me; I'm OG Snake, Blood; I'm loco or insane

Baby girl, I love you; you feel me; this I know
Don't ever play me, or like them haters, you gotta go
Baby boy, I love you too; we'll ride or die till the end
Blood in, blood out—please excuse me; I'm showing my demons

Back to the subject: you are what you eat
I've ate a little catfish, and a lot of cat I've beat
Push up on this puddycat or nut up if you dare
Atmosfear is between us; it's your fear; the atmos is only air

At-Must-Fear

You heard that silly saying: you are what you eat
I got a heart of gold; I'm a product of these streets
I've got that Midas touch, so I've been told
Everything that I touch is sure to turn to gold

I got a lot of love flowing through these veins
Haters have attempted several transfusions; all were in vain
Playa haters, beware; I go live and big off in this game
You know me; I'm OG Snake, Blood; yes, I'm loco or insane

Baby girl, I love you; you feel me; this I know
Don't ever play me, or like them others, you gotta go
Baby boy, I love you too; we'll ride or die till the end
Blood in, blood out—please excuse me for my demons

Back to the subject: you are what you eat
I've ate a little cat, and a lot of cat I've beat
Pet this pussycat; test me if you will
There's only at-must-fear between us; yes, curiosity kills

Miss Bee, I Itch

Miss Bee, do you have some calamine
I have an itch; I can't scratch in my heart and in my mind
I thought I had this hot itch scratched for good
I can't stop itching nor rubbing it, if I could

It started as a small benign rash
Now it covers my entire, don't ask
It's taken over my life—no, my well-being
This itch has not stopped me from seeing

What life would be like without an itch
I can't turn it on and off like a switch
No matter how hard I scratch, I'll never rub it out
In my heart and my mind, I itch and I shout

Miss Bee, do you have some calamine
To soothe this persistent itch of mine
Miss Bee, I itch deep down inside
Miss Bee, I itch, and this itch I have is not benign

Sated

Starving describes the way I feel most of the time inside
Deprived of nourishment needed to survive
I can't satisfy my appetite; my cravings are strong
Is being properly fed a crime? Is being sated wrong

At Mickey D's, I ate three happy meals and two orders of fries
My hunger persisted, and my starvation did not subside
I've been deprived of nourishment that not all food can provide
No matter how much I eat, I'll never be satisfied

I'm hungry and starving at the same time, if you know what I mean
Unlike Jack Sprat who ate no fat or his wife who ate no lean
I've ate the flesh, and I've eaten fruit from the forbidden tree
Knowledge of flesh is the nourishment needed to sate me

Sated by the acts preformed to procreate
Sated in the pursuit of and the knowing of a mate
I'm hungry and starving even though I ate
Feed me more, for goodness sate

Love's Biggest Fool

You know me; I am who I am
For you, I'd do anything that's anything I can
All you have to do is ask, and I'll give you my right hand
Are you sure you don't like green eggs and ham

I know you're busy; you'll see me when you can
I adore all things you; I'm your biggest fan
Thanks for my gift, just a little of your time
I'll treasure those moments as mine all mine

What can I do for you; I'll break the golden rule
You know me; I am who I am—love's biggest fool
You are the one, and you are in all of my dreams
You say you don't like green; life's not what it seems

Are you sure you don't like green eggs and ham
I want you to want me; I am who I am
Love's biggest fool, and for you I will surely do
Love's biggest fool, and I'm a fool for you

Talking It

Why do playa haters talk it
Saying da got so much paper, but all da do is spit
Da claim to have ah stable; some say da got ah herd
When ah real playa front um, not one can be heard
Claiming to be dah biggest tuna catchers, anyone could be
Like Charlie's canned tuna, dah best chickens of dah sea
Not one shows dah proper respect for dah queens of dah earth
Not one can recognize ah true woman's worth
There's no hero's welcome fo' rolling on
ah six-in-dah-morning creep
There's no glory in making dah final bed fo another playa's sleep
Once ya start turning corners, dah odds
are in dah favor of dem streets
Talking it and not living it is dah fastest
way to halt ah playa's heartbeat
Don't talk it if ya don't live it, and be prepared fo ah short run
Not every playa spitting it is talking it;
some spit is splatter wit ah gun
Talking it can leave ah bad taste in yo mouth
Talking it and living it guarantee yo ticket fo dah trip down south

Scroll Down

I have much to say if you will listen
Much has transpired without an explanation given
I'd like to plead my case; you are my judge
There isn't any reason to hold a grudge
Scroll down
I was caught up in the game; you got me twisted 'round
I lost control of my emotions, but now I'm found
Cataracts clouded my vision and my primary mission
I was wrong in my approach; that's a true confession
Scroll down
Let the dust clear from the air, and we'll pull up a chair
Clowns act a fool at the circus or the state of affairs
Pastures are greener on the other side of the fence
No Trespassing posted, I was invited; that is my defense
Scroll down
I have much to say if you will listen
Much has transpired without an explanation given
When you slow down, scroll down
I'm here for you; please forgive this clown
Scroll down

I Never Meant to Make You Cry

Wipe them tears from your eyes
I've never meant to make you cry
I'm a little rough around the edge
To you, I'll make this pledge

I pledge I'll think about you before I act
I'll consider your feelings first, and that's a fact
Life can be cruel, and it has so many rules
I'll treat you as my most precious of jewels

I know you're not able to be all mine
I'm content with just sharing a few moments of your time
Your attention is worth more than all of Fort Knox's gold
My feelings for you can't be measured or put on hold

I've made you cry, and it has taken its toll on me
You being unhappy, I never wanted that to be
Wipe them tears from your eyes
I never meant to make you cry

If I Were from Somewhere Else

I wonder how my life would be
If I were from somewhere else
Like from the dark side of the moon
Living in an underground self-contained cocoon

The first planet I'd visit to learn about its beings
The third rock from the sun would be worth seeing
I know there would be intelligent life-forms there
They've polluted the moon and their own atmosphere

I know that planet is the place for me
There is flowing water and polluted seas
Life's on the brink of extinction except for two or three
These earthlings call these survivors—endangered species

I wonder how my life would be
If I were from somewhere else
Outside of this polluted galaxy
The third rock from the sun, I really longer want to see

What If

What if you had never met me
How boring life would be
Or I had never met you
We never meeting would've been definitely taboo

Do you remember when we first met
Yeah, me too; where were we at
Me and you, you and I
I'll never forget you; I wouldn't try

I know I'm not ideal; my mood swings, they're far from idle
My personality ranges from domesticated to homicidal
I hate everything about nothing
I laugh at any and almost everything

What if you had never met me
How uneventful life would be
Or I had never met you
You are my salt, and you are my honeydew

Have I Overstayed My Welcome

Have I dallied too long
Have I overstayed my welcome
Your allure is not so strong
Have I done something wrong

We no longer see eye to eye
Hellos now sound like goodbyes
Everything I say annoys you
You no longer care about what I do

When you hear my name, you no longer smile
Our time together is less than a little while
Has my touch grown old
Your presence is a bit snippet; it's ice cold

When I reach for your hand, it's no longer there
When you see my face, you leave for fresh air
When we are together, I'm lonesome
Have I overstayed my welcome

Chess

Salutations exchanged, the introductions prior to the game
Seated across the table, I've already forgotten their name
The table is set, but dinner will not be served
"Which hand do you choose?" is what I've heard

Left or the right, each hand holds a black or a white
Will I move first or last, the first test in this plight
I'm in it for the love of the game, not for the fame
The first test is fruitless; my intentions are always the same

Conquest, domination, and a decisive clear-cut ending
Chess and life are games, and not all players are worth befriending
Most of them, I'll never repeat their name
Most leave confused, dazed, and amazed; some leave in shame

Salutations exchanged, the introductions prior to the game
Seated across the table, I've already forgotten their name
Toppled in their middle game, I always start my game at the end
Me, me, I checkmate foes as well as friend

That's Why

For the better part of my life, I've lived like a red
raging ram in a Chinese Tiffany china shop.
I'm like cream in black coffee; I always change
the flavor, and I always rise to the top.
I've never tiptoed through the tulips, nor
have I taken the time to cry.
I'll admit a drop or two have dripped from
the corner of at least one eye.
Damn, I wish I could remember when and why.
I've been told that my heart and my hands
were similar; they're callous.
I was told that my lifestyle was like a blind race-car driver
trying to win the Indy 500, reckless and careless.
I've always tried to make life do what it does so I can do what I do.
I never meant for my lifestyle to hurt you.
When I trip, I learn from that experience gained by the fall.
I climb to the top of every situation in spite of
the sudden stop at the end of it all.
I said all that to say this: I never meant to make you cry.
I just want you to understand who I am and why.

No Show

I woke up this morning only to find
You no longer want to be on my mind
I woke and watched the morning dew
I wonder who is dreaming of you

You denied me of my favorite dream
It's like having coffee without cream
Where did you go; I missed you last night
You never came as I wished you might

I woke up this morning, and you were not on my mind
I woke before the sun had a chance to shine
I watched the day break through the horizon
Morning dew sparkled and danced as the sun was arisen

My dreams of us need us, if you will
My heart bleeds; my mind stood still
You are loved; I want you to know
In my dreams last night, you did not show

Twenty-Twenty Vision

I envision and I dream of our future in full view.
Clearly, my future has always included you.
I have twenty-twenty vision, but my cataracts
make it hard for me to see.
I dreamed of you and of us as we, but your
dreams were beyond my ability.
When I woke this morning, the day was
clear as my mind and my view.
My dreams and visions no longer include you.
No, I'm not saying we are through.
I'm saying, in everyone's life, you must do you.
Us can never be one contender or one winner.
Us, that's me, myself, and I; and you as we is six degrees from center.
I need you for me, you know.
You—you're a no-show.

I Forgot to Tell You

I forgot, so I'm telling you now
It slipped my mind somehow
I must have gotten so wrapped up
Excuse me for this major hiccup

I meant to tell you several times
That mistake is mine, all mines
These three words I should have said
I'm not sure what was going through my head

Whoever said actions speak louder than words
Whoever said it never meant these words should go unheard
I never meant for you to go without
Hearing these words spoken softly and without doubt

I will tell the world without any reservations
You deserve a Taj Mahal; the world's greatest dedication
For you, there is nothing within my abilities I would not do
Damn, I think I've done it again; I forgot to tell you

You Knew

It was the night before
You walked through that door
You came in from out of the rain
Drenched from head to toe, covered in pain

Teardrops mixed with raindrops
Thunder crying nonstop
Weather like life is clear, then not
Life like weather is cold and hot

You sought shelter and comfort in me
Hurt feelings like stormy weather, eyes too cloudy to see
I am here for you; I am your shelter, armor, and shield
I'll provide for you when there are no crops in the field

It was not last night but the night before
You walk through that door
I have always been here for you
I am, and you knew

When Love Follows a Straight Line

When love follows a straight line
It looks forward as if blind
It leaves broken hearts by not looking back
I'll explain by the numbers, the *ABC*s, as a matter of fact

Zero loves one, and one loves two
Two loves three, who knew
Numbers and love sometimes confuse
The *ABC*s this time I'll use

A loves *B*; *B* loves *C*; *C* loves *D*
Love in a straight line happens relentlessly
Blinded by straight-line facts
Looking forward and never looking back

Look back for someone looking for you
Look back, then move forward after you do
When love follows a straight line
A true love may get left behind

I Never Complain, and I'm Not Rude

I have never complained about my attitude
I have never complained about me being rude
I have never complained about me being late
I have never complained about everything I hate

Complaining is just a waste of my time
Why write a complaint in verse and line
Lately my feet hurt, and my head hurts too
I'm not complaining because that's something I'd never do

Why come I never can get the best out of life
Why have I been plagued with every struggle and strife
I'm not complaining; let me remind you
I have never complained; that's something I'd never do

I have issues too; need I explain
You'll never ever hear me complain
I can tell you that's just one of my many virtues
Shut your piehole; I never complain, and I'm not rude

Will You Be My Valentine

Every moment of every day is our time
Please, tell me that you will be mine
Please, listen and feel what I am saying to you
Understanding how I feel, that is what I need you to do

Understand that our hearts should beat as one, not two
Understand that, for you, anything within my abilities, I will do
Feel the heat of the fire burning within my heart
Feel Cupid's arrow pierce and kindle our fire from a single spark

Neither time nor distance, woman or man,
can divide or keep us apart
My love is your bridge; the toll is paid; cross over into my heart
Your love, your heart, your touch, your smile, and your kiss
Yours is what I need to fulfill my Saint Valentine's Day wish

I am yours; please tell me that your mine
I love you through good and bad times
In my heart, true love you will find
Will you, my love, will you be my valentine

Clout

I have what others only get to dream about
I'm a mover and a shaker; the possessor of clout
I'm not referring to my backhand; it's a mighty blow
Not set tripping, idle wishing, or pimping, you know
Powerful influence, the power to push or to pull
Presence and self-respect, clout without all that bull
I turn pessimism to optimism; I'm more than nil or null
The glass was half-empty; now the glass is half-full

I'm like Jell-O when there isn't room for any more
There's always room for me; open up; don't shut any door
I have it, and I am it while others are doing without
Conner MacLeod, *Highlander*, said, "There can
be only one. I say never count me out"
Money, power, and respect are tools for a starter kit
Self-respect, strong presence, attitude—I never quit
When I step, you step; you know what I'm talking 'bout
Action or inaction, I can lead or follow; I possess clout

Dirty Red

A stormy night in a king-size bed
We lay exhausted, hum "Dirty Red"
Rain danced to the wind's song
Dirty red's always right; dirty red's never wrong

Passionate kisses are as intoxicating as red wine
Drunken monkey versus spitting cobra—martial arts, so divine
Thunder rumbled and screamed, "Do it all night long"
Dirty red is hot and spicy; dirty red is innate to the bone

Lightning illuminated every cloud in the sky
Dirty red could be seen from our eyes to our thighs
Lightning whispered, heightening our electricity
Dirty red is the ultimate amp; dirty red is unadulterated ecstasy

Fatigued yet ready, thoughts of you picturesque in my head
Last night, the only storm reported brewing was dirty red
Hot and spicy to the bone, the ultimate
ecstasy; rain danced to wind's song
Dirty red's always right; dirty red's never wrong

Lest We Forget

Teardrops blot and befall my eyes
Sold like cattle and swapped like flies
Millions dumped in the oceans, they never arrived
Millions beaten and dehumanized, few survived

Lest we forget our history
It's the story about you and me
Some are still lost at sea
They are the only ones truly free

I'll never forget family and great mother's hands
Influenced and molded the rough edges of this man
They told me of times before these streets
In the here and now, they're still wearing the sheets

Slavery is invisible now, but I still see the chains
The past and present litter with pain
Teardrops blot and befall my eyes
Sold like cattle and swapped like flies

Ain't That the Pot Calling the Kettle Black

When first said, I was taken aback
Ain't that the pot calling the kettle black
If I didn't know any better and was deaf in both ears
I'd have cause to question, to question what I hear

Don't open your mouth; words trip over your tongue
Water pressure bust pipes; me, I bust lungs
Speak when spoken to, and don't speak out of turn
Smokey the Bear lamented; you can stop
forest fires; when will you learn

When you live in a glass house, don't throw stones
With a glass jaw, an uppercut will lead to broken bones
Don't let your alligator mouth overtalk your hummingbird…not ask
Better than me take a look in the reflecting glass

I'm a sinner; I'm damned; I doomed in these streets
I'm going to hell in a hand basket; I'm a breath away, a heartbeat
When first said, I was taken aback
Ain't that the pot calling the kettle black

Can I Drive

Do you know where we're going or how to get there
You've been driving in a circle or a large square
Let's stop doing these Daytona 500 NASCAR laps
Our destination lacks a clear road map

Both of us can't drive this car
Our destination isn't far
I've tried my best to navigate
No matter how long it takes, we won't be late

Can I drive this car to a place called Destiny
It's in a little town called Ecstasy
We'll leave Lust and take a right into Compassion
We'll leave there and stay a few nights in Passion

I know where we're going; can I drive us there
You've been driving in a circle or a large square
Let's go to this little town in Ecstasy
Can I drive us to our Destiny

In December

It was sometime during the winter
The exact month, I vaguely remember
It was a cold day, so I think it was in December
My memories are jugated with excitement and splendor

It was the first time ever
I won't stop doing it, no, never
I was a youth; it was time, and I knew I should
My, oh my, it was more than good

It was warm and moist; I'll try to describe
How I felt when I finally got inside
I didn't rush right in; I took it real slow
I held onto both sides and entered all aglow

Hot, steamy, and wet, I eased into it—what a blast
I took my time; I didn't want it to end too fast
I felt really dirty, but I knew I would do it at last
I still remember that day; I took my first bubble bath

Hold the Rope

Hold the rope; the mule knows the way
You're a beast of burden; you will toil all day
Mind and body weary, you do you
Let your mule pull the plow; plant your seeds and follow through

Never give up; your struggles have only begun
Hold the rope; you do what must be done
Look behind you; see where you have been
A day at a time, the future is not a dead end

Dead ends are stumbling blocks for those
not determined to get ahead
Hold the rope; don't fall or give up; don't live among the living dead
Forty acres and a mule, an unfulfilled
promise not guaranteed to you
Point your mule in the right direction; it's
up to you to follow through

Hold the rope; the mule knows the way
As a beast of burden, it will toil all day
Plant the seeds you can live with, for they'll grow
Plow ahead; hold the rope; you reap what you sow

Paperboy for Life

I recall a time in the life when I won't give
Raised in the church, but I chose a life I couldn't live
Like Stevie Wonder, I'm looking back on when
I was a little, nappy-headed boy
I was killing time and never sharing my toys

Days and nights, in the streets is where I spent my time
A paperboy for life, forever on the grind
Looking left, then right, always looking behind
Before I crossed the streets into a life not so sublime

I never wanted for anything, for everything was mine
Hot Penny had no name; Nina stopped issues on a dime
I'm a paperboy who abandoned his route that doesn't forgive
I took a detour along the way; I chose a life I could live

When I won't give, I never lived, nor could I love for true
A paperboy for life, sanguine through and through
I recall a time in the life when I won't give
Raised in the church, but I chose a life I couldn't live

Life, What a Dangerous Game We Play

I live and learn each and every day
To our Lord, God, in Jesus' name, I pray
Tupac Shakur sang "To Live and Die in LA"
Life, what a dangerous game we play

Some inject into their veins and nod their lives away
Others smoke cigarettes at least two packs a day
Some smoke powdered or rock cocaine
They've chosen their poison; I'm not even trying to explain

Thousands have died as passengers on airplanes
Countless have succumbed to the tragedies of railroad trains
Wars have taken a many of souls to the other side
Life, like submarines and the *Titanic*, they've taken their fatal dive

In the game, we all do our best to stay alive
Select your poison and roll the dice; I pray we all survive
We live and learn each and every day
Life, what a dangerous game we play

Q and A:
Asked and Answered

Q and A: asked and answered—feet first
in pants, followed by the legs
"Do I love you?" is like asking which came
first, the chicken or the egg
To be wanted and cared for is desired; it's priceless
Isolated and ignored love is like starving oneself; it's senseless

"Do I love you?" is like asking, Why did the chicken cross the road
We all search for a greener or grassier grove
Sunshine is to moonlight as day is to night
Eyes are for seeing, but every eye doesn't have sight

Time measures, heals, and destroys like love; time is dateless
Dates mark, remind, and record like love; dates are timeless
A thin line between love and hate is drawn in the sand
It succumbs to the winds of change and the swiping of hands

The chicken came before the egg; it crossed
the road to get to the other side
Sunshine and moonlight, my love for you; I do not hide
I want and care for you; our time is sundown to sunrise
Q and A: asked and answered; I love you endlessly realize

I'm Crying

These aren't tearing eyes which have discovered secrecy
These moans aren't the sounds of a soul stricken by morbid misery
Sweat off my brow drips and drains into the corners of my eyes
Cut to the quick, no blood, no pain; me moan, I never cry

In the dark where secrets live and breed
They lie in wait; they ask to be retrieved
A word, a wink, a glance
Secrets are like mystery guests; who invited them to the dance

Knowing is like winning the battle but not the war
Blood, sweat, tears, and pain forevermore
Not every secret has to be known nor brought to light
Be careful for what you ask; day wears a mask at night

I'm crying, no, those are not tears you see
I'm crying, no, those moans are not sounds of misery
I'm crying, no, sweat drips into my eyes
I'm crying, no, cut to the quick; I never cry

Fasting

I'm starving for a taste of you
Fasting has me teary eyed, yes, misty blue
I miss your glazed, sugarcoated lips
I'm still hypnotized by the swaying of your hips

My eyes possessed by and locked between those…oh my
Creamy-white below, very voluptuous suckling on high
Hunger has drove me crazy; I needed to feed
My excessive desire for you is defined as greed

You knew I wanted you from the very start
You knew I wanted the largest piece of your heart
I still want you; you know that's not a lie
Teardrops are tatted for every moment lost under my right eye

Damn, you're constantly on mind
Your hugs and kisses would be so divine
I'm starving for a taste of you
Fasting has me teary eyed, yes, misty blue

Java Junkie Dreaming

Last night, when I did get some sleep
After tossing and turning between the sheets
I dreamed we were on fire like volcanic lava
I'm not sure why, but we tasted like java

I dreamed that we were a hot steaming drink
We were the coffee in a cup on the sink
I was the coffee; you were my cream
Mixed together, what an erotic dream

You were the coffee, and I was your cream
Mixed together, what a seductive dream
Hot as lava and tasty as java, in too deep
Coffee and cream in a dream as I sleep

Our sugar and our honey added to the mix
Caffeine junkie dreaming and craving a fix
Hot and sweet as a mocha latte; no, please don't stop
Like Maxwell House coffee, we're good to the last drop

I'm Powerless

I'm powerless; I'm saying more by saying the least
Relationship in your harbor stuck between west and east
Empty is my vessel far from being full
Adrift close to coming in, grab my rope and pull

Atrophy within my arms, my legs, and my hands
Unable to pull you close, I can barely stand
Deep within my heart, I sing this song
"Time is too short. Why is time so long"

I only want what is only yours to give
Only you can fill my vessel, and for you, I live
Pull me in closely; strengthen me from within
I'm powerless due to atrophy; on your strength, I depend

I'm powerless; I'm saying more by saying the least
Pull me into your harbor where west is one with east
Drop by drop, my vessel fills within you until it's full
Open your harbor deep and grab my rope and pull

A Duck's Life

Note how graceful a duck glides as it swims in a pond
How effortlessly it flies into the great beyond
Undetected turbulence underneath, it's kicking its feet
Unseen air resistance pressing on its head and beak

Watch as it struggles against current flow and tide
Turmoil below the surface swirling about on all sides
Winds are calm; they gust; winds of change forever blow
With ease, a duck soars aloft, flapping fast or slow

A duck's life in the skies and ponds, mine is much the same
I take life for what it is; I quickly adapt to life's game
No matter whether or the weather, never am I lukewarm
Surviving life's deceptive calm and its temperate storm

On the pond, I watch the ducks, and I ponder
Does a duck say, "Life's struggles won't take me under"
While flying high or treading water on life's pond
Like a duck, I'm facing life well into the great beyond

Two Heads Are Better Than One

Two heads are double the travesty or triple the ecstasy
Two heads are better than one; is that a possibility
One to plot or to plan, one to imagine or to dream
One to project or to exude, one to lambaste or to scream

When one sniffles, one is sure to sneeze
If one blew, one is sure to feel the breeze
Two heads are better than one; one could say it's so
One can always find the other where one chooses to go

Consequences and repercussions, one body and two heads
One must be the leader; one must be led
Questionable pleasures and adventures waiting to be done
Two heads are better than one

One is a thinker with the capacity to
deceive and the ability to perceive
Disastrous or pleasurable is a liaison in between dusk and dawn's eve
One blindly leading the one that can see
One thoughtless leading the thoughtful one to agree not to disagree

It Will Come to Light

What's done in the dark of night
Cowers to the flickering of a lightning bug's light
In black holes, neither sunlight nor truth escapes its vacuum
Sunlight and the truth are consumed
If done in the dark, it will come to light
Turn left into darkness; make a left to get back right into the light
In a dark room, photographs are illuminated via red light
Plots and uncover operations by candlelight
It will come to light out of the darkness of night
Unseen, unheard, and unsaid who might
See no evil, hear no evil, or speak no evil about tonight
Sneaking, creeping, or making moves and lining up the sights
Shadows don't cast in the darkness; all is shade
Lines are crossed; secret deals brokered, and beds go unmade
Lies and fears beyond yonder window break; the truth is born
When the light shines in the darkness, will it forgive, or will it scorn

Greatest Journey

Childhood to adulthood is a great distance to span
It's like a voyage on the open ocean from boy to man
A journey destined to come as night follows day
Facing internal and external challenges along the way

The greatest journey I've undertaken is between you and me
Measured, weighed, and balanced on feelings like waves on the sea
Tidal waves, surfs so lovely to see, and the occasional tsunami
I'll never disembark our ship, our voyage, our destiny

My greatest journey wasn't over an ocean or across any land
I've traveled to the North Pole, Europe, Asia, and Japan
My travels will never be more worthy than we to discuss
Land nor ocean mass has been compared to the distance between us

Closing that distance is the greatest journey I've undertaken
Time slips into the future, so I'm chasing the
greatest of our memory making
Moments that can be and that will be had between you and I
The greatest journey I've undertaken is between our eye

State of Mind

I think others can read my intentions when I know they can't.
I'm constantly looking over my shoulders as I pretend that I ain't.
I intend to be more than my intention, more than
the mere words I've thought to mention.
Truly a prisoner of my thoughts of the whys, of the
why not, the pleasures that copulation ought.
Somewhere trapped inside my head, there's a
conspiracy of words said and unsaid.
Wanting what's not mine, then having what's to be had.
My state of mind is sincerely bad.
Insight has double-crossed my mind.
I can't see, but I'm not blind.
My eyes wide open, yet misty sweet is the fog clouding my view
Of the sunlight coupling with the twilight,
twined as we couple in its dew.

Shame

Being in full regalia was a natural state of decency
Denial and finger-pointing turned natural into an obscenity
A woman and a man were the first to discovered shame
Covering it with leaves, neither would cull the blame

Show only me, your shame in its full regalia
Let me be the one to succumb to your beguile and galia
Born were we to indulge in our shame to the exclusion of all others
Who attempt to gander at what we share with one another

Your sweet melons are ripe, and your tulip blooms below
In a well-manicured garden for my pleasure, I know
Clothing veils us from peering eyes upon our privacy
Goggling at our shame of old, reserved for only you and I to see

My shame is not for the world to see; it
is for you, and yours is for me
Being in our full regalia is a natural state of decency
Denial created an obscenity and a natural ban
Our shame is the shame of the first woman and man

Scenic View

My eyes see you, and my heart bleeds for your beauty.
You've aroused my lust, and my love for you within me.
I love seeing the whole of you.
You're picture perfect; you're a scenic view.

Your lovely smile, eyes, breast, thighs, and hips.
I treasure the times I've kissed your lips.
Your beauty and being are worth a thousand words.
You're a sight to be seen and a musical pleasure to be heard.

You are the one, and you are all I'll ever need.
I'm hungry for you; I can only wish no other you'll feed.
Many covet your being, and many neglect how you feel inside.
Most will only want the flower blossoming in the valley of thighs.

Your feeling and thoughts have bloomed, and I enjoy your rose.
Your tulip I've picked, and your aromatic
scent is embedded in my nose.
You're my flower garden, and I will tend to you.
You're picture perfect; you're a scenic view.

Your Circle

I love you; my feeling for you I've spoken and wrote
My love for you is outside your circle; it's isolated and remote
I'm standing in the shadows; my love is like the sun blacked out
I'm on the outside of your circle, one foot
nearly in and both feet out

It's not a perfect world; love will not always prevail
Day and night, I think of you; my life is a living hell
Wanting and not having the best lover for me to be had
Pleasure is being with you; pain is you
ignoring my love; denial is sad

Who am I to start a riot and set my pains aflame
I know you loved another; I'm self-
inflected; I have only me to blame
Asked is my opinion, my counsel when you're blue
Truth from speculation, deciphered to reveal the clues

One day, you'll see my sunlight, and you'll realize
True love I have shown you, yet you close your eyes
I'm standing on the outside; I'm on the other side; I'm looking in
The world is not perfect, but I'll love until the very end

Masks

What are you doing while I'm doing what I do?
While I'm researching my heart's data, searching for a clue.
What am I looking for? You might wonder or ask.
I am searching my feelings or my masks.
We all wear mask, or so I have been told.
I've worn a number of masks from youngster to old.

I have special masks I wear just for you.
A smiling face, sparkling eyes, open ears hearing every
note of your voice as you say the things you do.
Wide open is my nose filled with your scent, your musk.
I'm craving you with uncontrollable lust.

I have another mask that I wear while I am worrying about your
well-being; it has a look of concern and a heartfelt yearning for you.
Know that, deep within my bones, I wear this mask
when I'm with you and when I'm alone.
The eyes of this mask reveal the depths of my
soul and my feeling that will never depart.
I call this mask "My Love for You"; this mask
is hung deep within my heart.

Just for We

There's a man with two heads, and both
heads have agreed never to disagree.
The agreement was unspoken, and it has caused much controversy.
The man had one body, and he was all but a reflection of me.
One head led but could not see.
One is always in love; the other is always looking for relief.
Both are looking for the ultimate state of happiness,
a utopia in a place known as "Just for We."
Well, let us not get too wrapped up in their
issues, which are less than a few.
My thoughts are littered with useless debris; there
might be something lying around you can use.
Take what I say for what you may because
I'm just throwing my thoughts out.
Most of the time, I'm dazed and confused, and
you have your own issues to work out.
Two heads are better than one, or is it? I sometimes have my doubts.

Gardener

Today, the sun was shining bright, and the sky was cloudless too.

I was looking over my flower garden; what a scenic view.

Nature is blessed with a many a splendid thing.

Snowcapped mountains and waterfalls that flow into valleys,
and into rivers were salmons swimming upstream.

I love tending my garden, and I love watching
the flowers grow just for me.

Life has made me a gardener, and now that is all I want to be.

Ghost Writer

On a starry night in a smoked-filled room
Good and evil met; the outcome—doom
One, a superhero; the other, you already know
It's the oldest story, and the plot of every show

From across the room, their eyes locked in a glance
It's the start of a failed romance
Forbidden love headed for travesty
It's the same old story told for a century

Every story has been retold
War and peace, young love flaming out in the cold
My stories, you've not heard them before
My stories happen in a room without a door

I'm a ghost writer; I write without paper in invisible ink
I write on the inside of eyelids; you can read my stories as you blink
Movie rights abound; Oscars and Emmys are claims to fame
Not for me, for I am a ghost writer; I have no name

Illusions or Mirages

In the heat of the desert, as well as in the heat of passionate
love, illusions or mirages play tricks on the mind. Objects are
closer than they may appear, for love is known to be blind.
The thin line between love and hate is more
than likely a circle of some kind.
Feelings and emotions circulate; they are intertwining as they bind.
Never give up on love because those mirages in
the desert or the illusions in passion may turn out
to be a real oasis, a real lover, a real find.
No matter what others think of you, you weigh heavy on my mind.
I see within you the good and the bad,
and I choose when to be blind.
My love for you is truly one of a kind.
The world is not a perfect place, but we are in it at this
moment in time, so while we are here, our love we'll bind.
Through all the mirages or illusions that play tricks on
my mind, you are a real treasure; you are a real find.

Do You Have Room

My heart needs a permanent home; can I come in
Can you provide shelter? Can you, my lover and friend
My heart is homeless; I'm lost out here in this world all alone
Do you have room? Can our hearts join
and form a place called home

It's raining in my world, and it's extremely cold
Flames from our hearts can warm us as we grow old
Can I come in? I'm on my hands and knees
Do you have room? Will you take me in please

My heart and I need a permanent home
It's raining and cold out here in a world all alone
Do you have room for me in your heart? It's such a large place
Do you have room for me? I do not take up much space

Do you have room for a heart that bleeds only for you
Do you have room for a lover, who is loyal and true
Do you have room for a friend, who will
be there through thick and thin
Do you have room for me in your heart? Can I come in

Don't Look Down

Keep your balance, your step, and your eyes on the other side
Face your issues head on; never run, and never ever hide
What goes up comes down, so make your stand on solid ground
When life threatens disaster, gloom, and doom, don't look down

While walking on the high wire of life
While facing personal struggles and strife
While standing on the edge of the highest cliff
Don't look down; don't doubt yourself with what if

What if there's no safety net
What if it rains on your parade and you get wet
What if the ground gives way, causing an avalanche
Don't look down; don't give what if a change

To cause you to slip and fall into uncertainty
Face down in self-loathing and obscurity
Don't look down; don't give up, and don't frown
Don't look down; keep your head up; don't lose your crown

Shelter

As I live and breathe, I've always kind of knew

Not to let the clouds in the sky block my heavenly view

When it's rainy, lightning, and thundering in my
life and things appear to be helter-skelter

I keep my head up; I'm not afraid of drowning
because Jesus is my shelter

Was I Wrong

I woke up this morning on the right of dawn
It was cool outside, morning dew on the lawn
Early birds were singing their early morning song
The sun had not shown its face, but it won't be long

Was I wrong to take my time to come to you
Was I wrong for living a life with a broad and unrestricted view
Was I wrong for being a prodigal child living just for me
Wrong was I; paradise lost and found, I was blind, but now I see

Skies partly cloudy, winds blowing calm
Paradise, not an island; trees, not palms
This place is where I truly want to be now and again
Where I am is not the beginning or the end

I can look backward and see the impressions I've left behind
I can look forward and envision new footsteps, yours and mine
I remember days when I wasn't sure which directions I should take
Broad was my direction; now my path is narrow, and so is my gait

Weighed and Measured

Broke or broken is the line, the measure, the sum
Who will be found lacking when all is said and done
Weighed, measured, and found standing in the cold
Broke or broken: life takes a heavy toll

The sum, nonetheless, time is no less or no sooner
Sixteen lines measure the length of a ruler
The weight of life is a yoke bared without a word spoken
Ongoing is the line; yes, time inches on unbroken

Broke or broken is the line, but it's not beyond repair
Learn from life by living through its fortune and despair
Broke or broken is not a place or a condition to be
Walk with measured steps, for nothing in life is free

Nonetheless is the sum of life's grief and treasure
Life inches in time; it's getting heavier with every measure
Weighed, measured, and found standing in the cold
Broke or broken: life takes a heavy toll

The Lie

I heard and saw the lie when it first walked in
It sought me out and claimed to be my friend
It said it spoke the truth and it was the light
Eloquently, it tried to convince me that day was night

I heard its sounds and felt the talons of the lie
Soft as a lover's whisper, painful as a hot needle piercing an eye
Sugarcoated words disguise the bitter taste of speaking
Its delivery was as gentle as a cobra spitting

Handless yet it shakes; its faceless smile a grin
Like Chucky, the lie said, "I'll be your friend to the end
"I'm your confidant. Confide and trust only in me
"Close your eyes. I'm your sight. You have no need to see"

The lie leads followers to a place I refuse to know
The lie walks the pit of Hades where it is sure to go
The lie says it's the truth for all to see and receive
The lie walks to and fro only to deceive

I'm Just Trying to Do Things Right

How I'm doing? You asked without hesitation
I know it's rhetorical; it's just another salutation
You don't really want to know how I'm doing
Pandora's box is open, and a storm is brewing

I woke three times in the middle of the night
Eight out of ten, surveyed like 7 Up over Sprite
Yesterday is much like the other day last week
I almost won the lottery; oh, that would've been sweet

I could've suffered a heat stroke; my aircon went out
I can get most stains out without Shout
Did you get six or twelve hundred for that tax relief
How have I been doing? Well, let me make this brief

If you really didn't want to know next time, just guess
I'm trying to do things right; I'm doing my best
Like Jack told Helen, ain't no telling; who knows I just might
Me, me, I'm trying to do things right

Back to Reality

I've often sat around during the day to dream
Going over all of the things I've imagined or seen
What if my illusions and dreams could come true
What if they did? I'd do all the things I wanted to

In the ocean, I'd want to ride
A seahorse of course; I'd jab it with my spurs in its side
In the fresh water, the legend of the deep of course
In the Loch Ness, I'd ride that prehistoric water horse

I'd want to be a cowboy but not the real kind, why
I've always wanted to ride a horsefly
Mobile homes are stationary; they don't even glide
I'd want to ride in a floating house or a housefly

I'd want to be a dragon slayer like those knights of old
I've slain a few dragonflies, should that story be told
Well, it's time for me to get back to reality
Back to my chicken farm where I raise chickens of the se

On the Other Side

On the mountains, in the valleys, and in the flats
Eyes see the climate changes, and eyes see the tragedy in that
Over here and over there are where eyes be
Observing it all, eyes saw all eyes dare to see

Occasionally, eyes wonder why it's happening there
Most eyes overlook the changes dangerously near
All eyes should be concerned about what's at hand
At the beach, more than a few eyes see more than sand

Eyes seeing in 3D and moving in slow motion
Eye sees more than the sea and less of the ocean
Eyes don't like what eyes see on the other side
Sore eyes seeing as they soar over the planet, as they glide

Weathered eyes see the changes in winter,
spring, summer, and autumn
Seasoned eyes gaze from the top and goggle to the bottom
Eyes see the earth's spectators and perpetrators of terracide
Sore eyes know that the grass is not greener on the other side

Unbearably Hot and Humid

Unbearably hot and humid, it's a blessing and a curse
Strenuous exercise suspended? The heat index at its worst
Exhausted and pleasured, we lie trembling, dripped with sweat
Mentally rehearsing all of the ways we know to get wet

We're hot and wet as Old Faithful; we're a natural work of art
When push comes to shove, our blood pressure stiffens every part
Our embraces culminate into drips and drops from crown to sole
Our explorations are extensive; we probe every hole

Red hot and burning from within, we blaze, then we simmer
Warmed by immeasurable pleasure, our bodies do glimmer
Picasso stroked the canvass so gracefully; masterpieces he created
We're a flaming-hot, wet works of art; our strokes go unabated

We'll lie here for a moment to air-dry our sweat
Unbearable is our heat; the humidity is hot and wet
Stimulated by fire and cautioned by the heat index
Unbearably hot and humid, it's a blessing and a hex

Hungry and Craving

Forever is my hunger, and it's you I want on my plate
I'm craving you as if I've never ate
Tender is your touch, and silky smooth is your skin
Well-seasoned is your body; you're a special blend

Hot and juicy, you're a feast in my famished dreams
Rare to the bone, lovely crimson and cream
Sweet as Mrs. Butterworth, dripping syrup on hot shortcakes
Your kisses, hugs, and loving—a fulfilling meal you do make

I'm craving you like a starving man; you're a feast, and I've not ate
I can't get enough of you; how much
longer must a hungry man wait
Let me taste all of your love; I'll be sure to clean my plate
I'm like Tony the Tiger; you're my breakfast, and you, you're great

Just one bite of you is a morsel, and for me, that will never do
Me, me, I'm a hungry man; I want an extra meal with desert too
Forever is my hunger, and it's you I want on my plate
I'm craving you as if I've never ate

Don't Be Fooled by a Trick

Never have I been the sharpest knife in the drawer
Nor have I been without need for just one more
Now and again, I've cut, and I've been cut to the quick
I'm saying this to say don't be fooled by a trick

Some tricks use smoke and mirrors to deceive
Disconnect—it's between the eyes and what one believes
A pretty face, bedroom eyes, and the illusive prize
How much time and effort spent, one must surmise

Is a trick worth one's consideration for its mysteries
Turn the cards face up; let all eyes see what my eyes see
The trick is there isn't a prize; the trick is
what is a sho'nuff fool willing to do
Egress now, for the prize isn't worth the price of the admission due

Keep it moving; there's nothing to see here but grief
I've seen tricks before, so I'll make my message brief
Never have I been the sharpest knife in the drawer
Nor have I been without entertainment;
so, trick, let's skip the encore

Little Red and Me

You got my nose wide open; need I hold my tongue
First off, you're a beautiful woman, fine and young
Little Red Riding Hood, the Big Bad Wolf is here
I'm naughty by nature, and I can taste your fear

I have a few thoughts; what are you willing to do
Play sheltered, but by night's end, you'll have a clue
I know all kinds of ways to have raw and naked fun
Best birthday suit contest, yeah, guess what? You won

Over and under, in and out, from here to there, we'll go
Little Red and the Big Bad Wolf going at it, you know
When all is said and done, we'll put on quite a show
I have a camera with no film; let's make memorable videos

My, what big…you have…it's better to…is it too much
You know me; don't be afraid to look and touch
What big ideas and big thoughts can I have, you ask
Little Red in red heels and me in my Big Bad Wolf mask

In My Way

Who's that standing at the door between you and me
No matter how close I get, it gets harder to see
When I move to the right, then left, you stand there stoically
You heard the knock upon the door; could it be for me

You're standing in my way between me and possibility
One knock and then the doorbell rang immediately
Move out my way, or answer the door for me please
Open the door right now before the caller leaves

Caller, the door is unlocked, and outside under the rock is the key
D——, I hope the caller heard my desperate plea
Why are you standing there? Excuse me; answer the call
Don't make me push and shove; one of us might slip and fall

Why do you stand there at the door and not answer me
You heard the knock; the doorbell rang,
and you did not open it to see
Oh no! I'm standing in my way; I'm
looking in the mirror, and it's me
Caller, please return; I've prepared myself for the opportunity

Can't You Tell

You've touched me deeply; can't you tell?
I've lived in search of heaven while here in hell.
It's fair to say I've been blessed to share a touch of heaven in you.
Your touches warmed a cold, dark heart,
and your touches are past due.

As I've aged, the days go by but not as they used to.
I find myself reflecting more on the joys of
life, like making love with you.
Reportedly, there is a land of milk and honey.
There is a land where love is not redeemed in money.

Here in hell, the cost of love has been high.
I've paid the price with a tear and a sigh.
A sigh of the relief and tear of joy because
I've known love here in hell.
In you, I've found love; can't you tell?

Beyond Compare

As the today turns to tomorrow, so the morn ends at noon
As the day turns to night, so the sun lights the moon
As the learned learn, their knowledge is not understood
As the bad gets worst, being bad means being good

As all good things too soon come to an end
As every race must start at some point to begin
As with gravity, what goes up also comes down
As crying is to laughter, a smile is to a frown

As addition is to added, one or more equals the sum
As teeth are to a mouth, chewing is to gum
As right is to left, right is to wrong
As less is to more, weak is to strong

As dated is to time, young is to old
As coal is to diamond, metallic is to gold
As thinking is to thoughts, being mindful is to care
As with everything, nothing is beyond compare

Present Time

Time has been the best and worst of my true friends
In time, in the meantime, sometime, time never ends
I've never held time or counted its grains of sand
I tried to hold back its hands, but time took my hands

I've look back on time to the remembered whens
I've look forward into time's abyss of what-ifs and then agains
Time is a gift; I'm opening it every day and right now
"What a present" is all I can say to life in time, "wow"

Life and times of the present, past, and future to be
Time-given lessons and pleasures of a wonderful family
Time teaches more than aging and less about being old
A lion's pride tempered, a fool's glitter pure as gold

If I could, I would do it all over just one mo'gin
If I had a head start on time, would time still win
Time is a teacher, the worst and best of true friends
The alpha and omega blessed me with
the present and the then agains

Three Wishes

Like *I Dream of Jeannie*, your body has granted me three wishes.
Sweet as honey, thick as molasses, and rich as chocolate kisses.
As I close my eyes and pinch myself, wow, you're here forever last.
Let's savor every moment and fill our noses with its aromatic blast.
The Young and the Restless are who we are *As the World Turns.*
We *Search for Tomorrow* every day; it's for each our heart's yearn.
We're on a *Fantastic Voyage* to *The Outer Limits* at *The Edge of Night.*
The Days of Our Life are quenched by
pleasures of each *Sunny Delight.*
Hold my hands gently and look deeply
into the windows of my soul.
You'll see an eternal fire burning for you, so you'll never be cold.
As the world wildly spins even when chaos has lost its control.
Pull me closer, love; embrace me tightly;
one upon the other, we'll hold.
Hotter and sweeter than Mrs. Butterworth dripping over pancakes.
Our love is tempered by your banana split and strawberry shake.
Sweets for my sweetheart, passionfruit and red wine for our souls.
Our age may run off and leave us, but our love will not grow old.

It Can't Be Bought

Don't look in the mirror for what's lost
within you, for it can't be found.
Images are reflected and reversed; it's the truth turned round.
Step into the mirror to seek those things unseen yet sought.
Inner peace is only a portion of the answer; it can't be bought.
One has to live within the confines of one's own heart and mind.
Insight is the portal for all inner vision, for without it, one is blind.
Foresight is for dreamers and seers of what one could be in time.
Hindsight is twenty-twenty vision, an afterthought, a look behind.
One's conscience is the blackboard chalked with every deed.
One lives happily or dies in misery as one
reviews their own humanity.
The image reflected in the mirror is the truth, or it may be the lie.
The image is real, but the answer isn't revealed to the naked eye.
Only one has the answer, and only one can step inside.
To seek what's sought by looking in the
mirror is better left to the blind.
Step into the mirror to seek those things unseen yet sought.
Inner peace is earned through selfless deeds; it can't be bought.

I Want to Know

I want to know; do you
I want to hold you in the morning's dew
I want your audience, your attention
I want something we dare not mention

I have been dealt these cards in hand
I can only play just who I am
I want to be your fantasy
I want to be the main ingredient in the us of we

If we dance the dance as we must
Will there be more than just the smell of musk
Will we find what others can only dream
If I come with ice, will you come with cream

I promise to do you no harm
Comfort can be had, one in the other's arms
Knowing you is what I want to do
We'll come together as we knew

Broken Dishes and Jack

I was there when they broke up
Yes, I'm talking about the saucer and the cup
The cup displayed a small but noticeable chip
No matter what was poured in it, it held its lips

The saucer was emotional; it had a hairline crack
It was more than a little crazy, but here are the facts
That day, I understood why Jack jumped over the candlestick
He was nimble; he was quick; he won't wash dishes; he did lick

Well, on the same day sometime in the afternoon
The fork and the saucer had an argument over the spoon
The fork heard the spoon, cup, and saucer had a few hot toddies
The three were with Jack, and the fork said, "You
three will regret getting wet without me"

The spoon hit the cup; it chipped; the cup hit the saucer; it split
The fork got stuck in Jack's tongue; he had to run to remove it
I was deep in the cut with the knife; we were
on edge; we never got into the fight
Like I was saying, they broke up, and I was there that night

Who Will Remember

Who will remember a playa's name
When all is said and done at the end game
When the last cards are dealt and the last dice are rolled
When day and night lose their way and Father Time folds

Who will remember a playa's name
The question begs to be answered without shame
Who will shed a tear? Who will sincerely miss? Who will fade
Who will pay a playa's dues on a bet finally made

Who will remember a playa's name
Every playa pays the cost to play; what's the price of fame
Some legacies, in this game called life, are priceless, not free
Heroes are memorialized; they've all paid a fee

Who will remember a playa's name
A playa not remembered has only oneself to blame
Who will remember a playa's name and a playa's legacy
Playas are never forgotten by true friends and family

Looking for Me

As I walked from here to there and back again
I'm not sure where I started or where I'd end
I passed by, then I had to pass by just one mo'gin
I'm looking for my lover, my companion, and my friend

My lover and I, we melt one into the other's embrace
My companion and I, we respect one and the other's face
My friend and I, we accept one and the other's flaws
Deep in you, looking for me, we have all three; let's pause

Looking for me deep in you as one entity
Looking for me, I've looked for you for an eternity
My eyes were closed as I searched from here to there
My mind was wondering if you were anywhere

As I walked from here to there and back again
I'm not sure where I started or where I'd end
I found you looking for me deep within
I found my lover, my companion, and my friend

My Favorite,
If It Needs to Be Said

Brick, crimson, vermillion, sanguine, ruby, cherry, and blood red
Every shade and hue, if it needs to be said
A rainbow is promise made by God to man
Red is its first color seen over water and land

Red flows freely through my veins
The red plant is beautiful, especially when it rains
Rage is an emotion, and seeing red is to blame
Red is passion and a fire's flame

There are so many from which one could chose
If it weren't for red, the world would sing the blues
Red is alive and well, red if it needs to be said
Without blood means without life; without life means to be dead

Blood red, cherry, ruby, sanguine, vermillion, crimson, and brick
So many shades and hues from which to pick
My favorite if it needs to be said
My favorite is the many shades and hues of red

We Know, We Knew

We knew it was that time
We knew, for some, one must wait
We knew, in moments, we are us; and we say each is mine
We found each other none too late
I'm hungry for you; have you ate

One are we together
Flocked like birds of a feather
Never to be plucked apart
Clasped like hands holding the other's heart
We have more than some could wish
Lips joined, minds connected, hips thrust as we kiss

Love me for true, and I will love you
Together we will make life do what it does
So we can do what we do
Nothing can ever be like it was
We know; we knew

Master Builders

A master builder is what I really want to be.
I'd erect monuments; I'd create works of majesty.
With my hands, heart and mind, I'd create splendors.
Standing the test of time, enduring summers and winters.

Between us is a distance; we're near yet sometimes too far.
I'd build a bridge to reach you no matter where you are.
Let's build this bridge with firm
communications built on solid land.
Our bridge will slip, sway, and collapse if built on shifting sand.

Let's lay our foundation on trust, not in doubt, suspicion, or fear.
The strongest bridge can topple under the weight of a single tear.
Meet in the middle, the half point of our minds,
our hearts, our outstretched hands.
There we will couple; over an ocean of confusion, there we'll band.
Master builders are what we truly ought to be.
Building a bridge between us, spanning the deepest of seas.
We'd create the most majestic and the greatest of all splendors.
Our creation will stand the test of time,
enduring summers and winters.

Young Pup, Old Dog

Young pup, come close to hear and learn about that pussycat.
Don't spend a lifetime chasing it; be careful;
some catch that dirty rat.
Grab a milk bone, young pup, and grab this old dog another deer.
Sit down right next to me and lend this old dog your ear.
Chasing cat is like chasing after your own short tail.
You'll be dizzy; you'll catch a few cats by the tail to no avail.
Not all pussy is the same; some will change the name of the game.
Dogs eat cat; cat eats rat; some pussy will eat a dog without shame.
Pup, being a big dog does place you at the top of the food chain.
Some cats will choose the rat, leaving you
chasing your tail in the rain.
Young pup, you can kill the pussy, but not
all pussy can or should be ate.
A dirty rat that cat has been catching may carry
the plague to your bowl like plate.
It's only natural, young pup, for the dog to chase the pussycat.
It's only natural, young pup, for the pussycat to chase the rat.
Listen up, young pup; this old dog can
teach you a new trick or two.
Kill the pussy; never let a dirty-rat-chasing
pussycat make you dizzy or kill you.

Standing on the Line

Standing on the line between love and hate, take a leap of faith.
Standing between right and wrong, one suffers little or great.
Standing for nothing is a slippery slope, where the fallen fall hence.
Standing for and not against, stand on this
side or that side of the fence.
How does one make a stand when deciding to eat after one has ate?
When does one say enough is enough,
don't pile any more on my plate?
Humpty Dumpty sat on the wall between
what's real and what's fake.
He was not for or against a fence, and good
neighbors a fence does make.
There's a thin line drawn in the mind
between what one is willing to take.
If the choice is to love or hate, suffering is
left of right, what's to debate?
One must decide one's own fate; one has a
choice that only one can make.
Decisions have a price, and indecision is paid at a hefty rate.
Falling in or falling out of love means crossing the thin line.
Heavy on the heart is the weight of love,
and hate is heavy on the mind.
Standing on the line between love and hate, take a leap of faith.
Standing between right and wrong, one suffers little or great.

Slip and Slide

By special request, come play on my toy; come, hurray, hurray.
Come ride, come slip, come slide, come parlay.
My "Slip 'N Slide" is fun to ride both night and day.
Free admission! Did I mention you never have to pay.

My toy is best when you get it very slippery and wet.
I know you know it's hard to "slip and slide" on a dry play set.
Natural or artificial, whichever you'd prefer to apply.
Moisten my toy to get it ready for a short or a long ride.

Slip down or glide until you're firmly seated at its base.
Slide up and down, fast or slow, the depth will regulate your pace.
There's no season, and there's no reason not to come copulate.
"Slip and slide"; fly high and glide; oh,
no, Premature E. Jack, you late.

Come ride my "Slip 'N Slide"; by special request, come play.
You'll have the time of your life; no, you don't have to pay.
Ride it fast or slow, night or day, up and down like an escalator.
My "Slip 'N Slide," you can come ride it now than later.

Limited Vocabulary

I have to apologize in advance for my ever-so-limited vocabulary.
My grammar is also lacking, so thank goodness for dictionaries.
I often regret not taking time out to proofread.
One has to decipher and translate what's what to halt or to proceed.

Now that I've gotten past that and you've continued on with me.
It's apparent to me that you've decided to accept my apology.
I write my thinks and thoughts of a world
passing by me at Godspeed.
Others have fed on all things read, and I've
just now been seated to feed.

I want to express, but the few words I pose fail to paint the scene.
I want to explain, but then it rains washing
away; what was the theme?
The other day I wrote to say how much I loved you for the way.
But the words could not relay what I wanted them to portray.

Although I want and I need you to
understand my thoughts, I think.
Drunk on words, the things not heard are clearer after a cold drink.
My vocabulary is bad; my grammar, just as
sad; you understand what I mean?
Words fail beyond compare to say I love
you, and you fulfill my dreams.

When the Salt Has No Flavor

It's time for me to leave; I'll be around.
Derided by some, my spirit unbound.
I'm out of here when the salt has no flavor.
I'm blessed and highly favored.

The time approaches soon.
The sun smote the moon.
The season lost its salt.
Flavor never regained as it ought.

Time has ticked for every tock.
Clocks keep time like a shepherd keeps a flock.
Exodus, leaves, departs, unblemished without spots.
Did I say when or where I'm going? I'm sure I did not.

I have no regrets, none as of yet; enigmas I'm beset.
Questions beg to be answered, and I'm the usual suspect?
It's time to spice things up; it's time to savor.
I'm leaving when the salt has no flavor.

But I Don't Have a Costume

I want to be a superhero, but I don't have a costume.
I've been watching TV, reviewing the old and new cartoons.
I've studied the various characters, but
which one should I aspire to be?
All heroes have a mission to save our world;
it's a helpless and an immoral society.

Their incredible, exceptional powers
exponentially expended and hurled.
I'm smart, strong, and sensitive with a big
heart; and I want to save the girl.
Like Superman saves Ms. Lane and Tarzan saves Miss Jane.
But not like Captain Save-A-Ho saving tricks, playing mad games.

Should I wear a cape and spandex? Should I fly or run?
Should I have real or imaginary powers? Should
I carry a hammer or a shotgun?
This superhero business is not for the faint of heart.
It's frocked in tremendous trials and
tribulations in a world torn apart.

If I only had a costume, I could save the world from certain doom.
Batman and Spider-Man sweep up crime waves like they're brooms.
I've been watching TV, reviewing the old and new cartoons.
I want to be a superhero, but I don't have a costume.

Fishbowl

In a fishbowl, there it was circling; there it was confined.
A colorful fish was swimming; it had truly lost its mind.
It splashed the water as a signal, as a wave
for me to turn my eyes and head.
I had to listen closely, and this is what it told me; this what it said.

You and I have a lot in common; we were captured and enslaved.
You've been fooled; you think you're free, so you can never be saved.
Living in a society that counted you out
before you had a chance to start.
You are not expected to amount, never to
be a finisher, only a false start.

I said, "You know me not, you. I'm destined to succeed.
From birth, I can grow like a mustard seed."
"No," it said, "only if you purchase me, and then are
so kind as to take me to the ocean to be freed."
I understood what it meant; I understood what I
had to do; that was I had to make a stand.
All fish should be freed from fishbowls, and their
minds should be equal like those every man.

I protested; I picketed from the ark to the arch.
A fish had stirred the water in a fishbowl,
and the world began to march.
A fish was purchased and freed; no longer was it
enslaved in mindless ignorance on display.
One fish caused a ripple, causing a tidal wave; that's
eroding the shores of mindlessness every day.

Word Rage

I'm leaving my mark on this one of many but just this one page.
Read it carefully; each mark is the mark
I mark with a stroke of rage.
Each letter was slammed with a hard thrust to where you see it lay.
Never to be removed, it's embedded here till this very day.

Listen, I have a message with no kindness found.
Each word I'm writing is a clear challenge;
me, me, I'm ready to throw down.
Anger has manifested its ugly red head between,
in, and on each and every line.
Open your eyes; they're wide shut; it's in
braille for those who're blind.

I'm inking this page with marks no one will ever forget.
It's inked, and it's inscribed with letters
and words filled with disrespect.
So bitter the words burn any tongue that dares to speak it.
Your mouth will taste like stinking hot sh——
it will never be the same after.

I've inked the letters and words on this page.
Each line scrawled in measured strokes to
ensure no one missed the rage.
I'm leaving my mark on this one of many but just this one page.
Read it carefully; each mark is the mark I
mark with a stroke of word rage.

Green Eyes

She looked at me, longing to know, to have, and to be.
Everything that I had or would have, she wanted from me.
She cozies up to me, and that green-eyed monster smiled with glee.
She asked me did I have any dreams and
if so could she have a look-see.

She smells happiness and success with her
forked tongue; she doesn't breathe.
She laughs the laughter aired with deception; listen to her seethe.
She looks me in my eyes as she shakes my hand.
Her knives, she sticks like acupuncture needles
into my back whenever she can.

Don't get it twisted; Green Eyes is not a woman; I call her she.
Green Eyes, she's a hermaphrodite; she's
whomever she likes, and I do mean he.
Disguised in her "I care about you. Trust me" suit.
She wants my hard earned; she's not sated with just only my loot.

She wants what's deep inside; she wants
me naked and lacking pride.
Envy, jealousy, and hate on her plate.
She not an ordinary killa; she'd prefer one to commit suicide;
She's a whale eater feasting on yours and mine.
She'll swallow one whole and eat one's soul.
She's Green Eyes—envy.

Village Idiot

The village idiot, don't ask me; you'll see.
An idiot may or may not have lost touch with reality.
They entertain us when the circus has left town.
An idiot may take his act on the road as an unpaid clown.

Someone always witlessly runs for the village idiot of the year.
The elections are official, and the village
idiot status is held so sincere.
Wide is the path of the idiot, and endless are his predicaments.
Common sense is the ingredient lacking in all of his judgments.

Tripping over the same rock in his path, left
or right not in the same place.
No mirror can reflect enough light for him
to see the shame on his face.
It's a miracle; the idiot has not gone extinct like the dodo bird.
God protects babies and fools, or so that's what I've heard.

Don't study on it for too long, and never wonder or ponder who.
If you won an election you didn't run for,
well, it might be…no, not you.
The village idiot, don't ask me who; you'll see.
An idiot may or may not have lost touch with reality.

I Wasn't Told

I wasn't told, so I didn't know not to run with scissors in hand.
As a young child, I crawled, I walked, and I ran as fast as I can.
Never have I been one to think past the pains of everyday.
When running with scissors, I was stuck by the needle in the hay.

I was told not to stick the knife in the wall socket.
I was told not to shoot my friends with my wrist rocket.
Never have I been one to think of ways not to play.
When running with scissors, I was stuck by the needle in the hay.

I was told not to cut off my nose to spite my face.
I was told always to be thankful and before I eat to say grace.
Never have I been one to think of how way leads to way.
When running with scissors, I was stuck by the needle in the hay.

I wasn't told, so I didn't know not to run with scissors in hand.
I've tripped; I've fallen; I've stumbled; I've
had several great falls as I've ran.
Never had I been one to think about the lessons of yesterday.
When running with scissors, I was stuck by the needle in the hay.

Nappy Dugout

Some will never truly know what I'm talk'n about.
Some can only wonder while others pray to find out.
I've been around the play'n field, a time or
two; and me, me, I've got no doubts.
There's no place on the field like the Nappy Dugout.

As a true playa of the game, I love play'n the sport.
If one hasn't been in, one truly plays life too short.
One has to be in it to win it, to seal the deal.
A playa has to score to get in; me, me, I'm just keeping it real.

Playas in the infield and in the outfield
can't wait for their turn at bat.
They know like I know; the Nappy Dugout is where it's really at.
It's where all the playas come from, and it's from
where all the playas pay their dues.
No matter how hard or how long one plays
the game, no other dugout will do.

Batter up, batter on, batter in, and batter out;
all go back to the Nappy Dugout.
Some will never know what I'm saying; they've literally struck out.
I've been around the world, a time or two;
and me, me, I've got no doubts.
There is no place on earth like the Nappy Dugout.

Does It Matter in the Scheme

Whether or not I have or I have not a choice,
does it matter in the scheme?
Yes, I must make my own choices; that's life's theme.
Live one day at a time with my sights on the next day.
Open or closed, life will make a choice per se.

If I don't open the door, I won't know what's on the other side.
If I don't open the box, I won't know what's on the inside.
If I don't close my eyes, I won't know the power of dreams.
If I don't close my mind, I won't know life is not what it seems.

What if I open the door? Will I be ready for the things I'll see?
What if I open the box? Will I release beast that destroys reality?
What if I keep my eyes open? Will I not hallucinate eventually?
What if I close my mind? Will I live in ignorance perpetually?

So I must open the door, if only for a moment in time.
So I must open the box, if only for a moment to ease my mind.
So I must close my eyes, if only for a moment to dream.
So I must open my mind, if only for a moment
to know if what's what is as it seems.

The House I Built

Before I could enjoy my labor, the high tide swept it out of reach.
I built my sandcastle during the low tide on a private beach.
Yellow and red, soft and fuzzy, juicy and
sweet, I sowed the Georgia peach.
Johnny Appleseed was a good man, but he lied to one and to each.
It took several years and two tears in a bucket;
life is too short and too hard.
I built my home on the Great Plains with
a single deck of playing cards.
Since I can't have my cake and eat it too, I
concerned myself not, so disregard.
I left the cake out in the rain; and the recipe, well, I did discard.
Paul Bunyan, what a tall tale; now me, me,
I'm for real; I'm flesh and bones.
I built my log cabin with an ax and an ox
in a big city of bricks and stones.
Money doesn't grow on trees or in a booth called a pay phone.
I have all the money I'll ever need thanks to
my real friends at Payday Loans.
On cloud nine, I sleep on a bed without
pillows and without bedsheets.
I built my house on the stairway to heaven
on the sunny side of the street.
If you should happen by the house I built,
welcome is the mat, so do wipe your feet.
I've never met no one or everyone, and I'm
sure whosoever I'll never meet.

Apprehend My Ultimate Plan

How long will it take to understand the
intentions of other's ultimate plans?
This question lingers like the smell of death on the breath of man.
Scribbled on scrolls, some spoken by and some
told, and all are akin to scrabble.
Appurtenance of the word is the intent of what's
meant; intent's adjunct is babble.
The link is between what's said and what's
meant; the intent is yet to be unraveled.
Who loses and who wins is often hammered
out on hardwood with a gavel.
To walk a mile in another man's shoes is an uncertain
journey through what another has traveled.
So is a mile the measure in the footsteps of understanding
a paved road or a road that is graveled?
If what is said was always what is meant,
it would surely be the intent.
If what was intended were never amended,
then understanding is surely irrelevant.
"Seize the moment" means to apprehend the day;
the intentions of the meaning is evident.
"In a minute" is time spent between action
and delay, or is that a moment?

Judge not, lest you be judged by the same
measure and weight of your hand.
Understanding the intentions amiss the foul
odor of words has always plagued man.
In a minute, seize the moment, my intentions—
one may come to understand.
In a minute, is all the time it will take to
apprehend my ultimate plan?

Mama, When I Wake

Mama, when I wake in the morning, you may be gone
Don't worry 'bout me; am I right or wrong
Who knows, you may wake and not find me
I'm not here or there, so don't search beyond the old oak tree
I have all that I need to see me through
Don't worry 'bout me, nor will I worry 'bout you
Sure, I'd love to tag along to see what really goes on there...
Come visit me as often as you'd like; you're always welcomed here

Mama, you're my lady; yes, I love you; I'll never quit
You carried me; you cleaned me; you lovingly dealt with my sh...it
Hold me, as I hold you deep within my soulful heart
Mama, when I wake, you may not be here; but we're never apart

Thank you for your love I carry within me
Thank you for the wisdom shared, the lessons
learned, 'twas blind, but now I see
Thank you for the memoirs and the visions and dreams
Thank you for showing me life is not always what it seems
Mama, when I wake in the morning, you may be gone
Don't you worry 'bout me; am I right or wrong

In a Minute

"In a minute" is like saying "I'll see you one mo'gin"
"In a minute" is the duration of time; it has no beginning or end
"In a minute," unlike goodbye, it doesn't prophesize
In a minute, we will meet one mo'gin, and that's not a lie

Don't say goodbye to me as we depart company
Don't cloud my eyes with a gloom-and-doom type destiny
Goodbye sounds like a prediction of a long good night
When you leave me, please don't turn out the light

Should we never see or hear from one to the other one mo'gin
In our hearts and minds, we'll visit the memories
of us, my family and my friends
Remember the good times we had; remember some were even bad
Remember being glad; damn, them memories;
sometimes, I made you mad

In a minute, we'll share a moment or two
In a minute is when next I'll see you
In a minute, it's my way of not saying goodbye
In a minute, we'll meet and greet one
mo'gin; is that you…hello and h

Who Ate My Candy

Candy is like a beauty lady with its special flavors
She's forever sweet and never wavers; butterscotch
is just one of the many tastes I favor
It's just enough to savor; I love a Bit-O-Honey
Sweet, smooth, and sunny; on her, I'd spend all my money
There's nothing on earth like my Peppermint Pattie
She screams for her Sugar Daddy, if the story needs to be told
I'm thinking 'bout my Tootsie Roll; she's mouthwatering delicious
Red Hot Tamales, she starts my fire; she's so viciously malicious
My candy, I remember them all
There's not one flavor I can't recall
Now my sweets are nowhere to be found
So why are these candy wrappers lying around
Who ate my candy
When I find out, there'll be a retreat
In the middle of Sugarcoated Street, for
the sweetest candy you'll ever eat
Me, me, I've never gotten a cavity from my sweets
I guess one could say one man's candy is another man's treat

Your Flower, Your Rose

How do I nurture your flower
How do I get your nectar
How do I pick your rose
How do I maintain your aromatic scent in my nose

Little Sally Saucer sat there wiping her eyes; she didn't know
Little Bo Peep talked about her sheep, the ones she lost in the snow
Old Mother Hubbard talked about herself and Ole Rover's bone
Jack and Jill, well, they did talk about it;
they just want to be left alone

How do I nurture your flower
How do I get your nectar
How do I pick your rose
How do I keep your sweet smell in my nose

Tell me, rose; I truly want to know
Blossom for me, rose; let your petals show
Let me see your beauty unfold
You're a mysterious flower; you're a wonder to behold

Will You

Will you open up and let me in
Will you embrace me as more than a true friend
I'm knocking at the door; I'm ringing the bell
Your door mat reads welcome; is that to heaven or hell

Do you hear me knocking at the door? Do you hear the bell
I'm offering love; I'm not selling misery or a living hell
Come share you with me, and I'll share me with you
Let me in, then lock the door behind us, and we'll do what we do

Am I an unwelcomed salesperson who keeps dropping by
I'm not selling dreams; I'm offering shares
in my world under my sky
Greet me at your door, and I'll take you outside
Tour my world under my rainbow sky; come, come let's ride

Let's find that pot of gold at the end of the rainbow
Let's get wet in the Fountain of Youth and watch each other grow
Let's catch Cupid and shoot each other
with his arrows using his bow
Let's make our bed with flowers so we can reap what we sow

Love Loves

Love loves no one else; let me clarify: love loves itself
Secret spells and magic potions are useless
utters, and snake oils for a fool's shelf
Love can't be conjured up at will even though
it's often a self-manifestation
Love is the greatest form, if not the purest form of self-emasculation

Love is a story that's perpetually told
Love is her story and his story of new times and times of old
Love is the calm and the troubled waters running hot or cold
Love is priceless; it can neither be bought nor sold

Love lives in a blessed heart and in a kindred soul
Love is an inheritance of the meek, and it's taken
for granted by the proud prided bold
Love is to be reciprocated, but more often
than not, it's nonreciprocal
True love is clear as a flawless diamond;
it's not as green as an emerald

Love is abstract, yet it's as real and solid as concrete
Love is to live for; love is to die for; love can
conquer, and love can suffer defeat
Love can be felt while remaining untouched; love like a heart bleeds
Love doesn't love; love loves vicariously
like a fire as it feeds and breed

I Drowned the Rain

Don't look at me like that…it's a fact
Don't doubt my word…it's not absurd
Note the power of my left to my right; me,
me, I always put up a good fight
Know that it's unknown when the winds of change will blow
Well, when the winds blew, I knew it couldn't fade my seven or eleven
It came on like a great flood; it was after my blood
It hit me like a blackjack; it hit me dead in the center of my back
I wasn't dazed; my eyes weren't glazed; and me,
me, I was hardly amazed by its haze
As we fought, I thought I started to sweat;
and yes, yes, I did get a wee bit wet
I said to me self this is a test, so I made my next move, my best move
Premeditated, no, I never hesitated; I don't need an umbrella
The rain, yes, the rain, it tried to drown a fella
I fought it and shrugged it off as only I could;
you and I both know I'm just that good
Drenched but quenched by the world's stresses
and strains, me, me, I drowned the rain
It dripped; it splashed; it struggled, but I subdued
it and beat it into a mud puddle
I popped that festering purulent bubble
Like I said: I got a wee bit wet; me, me, I had worked up a sweat
I drowned the rain, worked through the pain;
you heard me; my word it's not absurd
It's a fact, and there's no need to fade me or to bet;
I drowned the rain, and I didn't get too wet

She's Unhappy With

Look at the way she smiles with reservations
A smirk comes first, then a smile comes after a belated hesitation
She unhappy with your brand of just us
served up without her just due
She's unhappy with you
Bonds, once bound so tight daylight couldn't
break through, have unraveled overnight
Dual visions, precise precisions, and coupled insights
are now dueling divisions and plights
When it rains, it pours on the promises of a forevermore
The relationship is wrecked on two distant shores
She's unhappy with the current events of the day
She's unhappy with the time and money not spent on foreplay

Jack and Jill, at the apex of their thrill, tripped
and fell out over a little water spilled
Bonnie and Clyde, what hell of a ride; they
knew their faiths were sealed
She says nothing is wrong; um, you know then nothing can be right
You were Sir Lancelot before chivalry was pronounced
dead; she unhappy with you, Good Knight
She's unhappy with the constant division;
she's unhappy with her final decision
She's unhappy with the speculative outlook, and
you the main character of her life's book

I Said

A closed mouth doesn't get fed; a blind eye doesn't see
Express yourself and keep one eye on your surroundings
Light illuminates the eyes and fulfills…so on that light do feed
If one has an alligator's mouth and
hummingbird's as…eat sesame seeds
I said what I said not to get in your head

I said what I said for one to heed, not just read
If you want it, ask; if you desire it, wish; if you need it, plead
Truly is blessed the one who has their own;
truly blessed is that one indeed
Oversight is not overlooking; the blind
lead the blind through illogic
What appears to be and what is can be viewed
by the misled as magic or tragic

Greed, need, or hunger determines whether
one holds fast or one takes a push
A bird in the hand isn't always better than two in the bush
I've said nothing to mislead or cause one to go amiss
Well, what I said doesn't amount to much about this

Some don't believe fat meat is greasy
Life is too short, and pimpin ain't easy
If you don't believe what I said, ask Jack Sprat
He never chews the fat; he spits only the facts on this or that

Your Biggest Fan

I don't think you heard me clapping my hands
I'm sure you did not notice me, me, your biggest fan
You don't have to be a superstar in the big
picture show on the movie screen
This maybe TMI, too much info, but while
I'm sleeping, it's of you I dream

Flour and water, my face adds in the mix blended into a crowd
I'm just another lonely raindrop released from a heavy cloud
If only I could be that drop of water that quenches your thirst
Or that drop of rain that rinses away the dirt and its worst

Let me build a dam of smiling faces to block a
single teardrop from marring your eye
Let me free your love from its cage, I'll teach your love to fly
Nothing short of my all, I wouldn't do
for you without reason or why
I'm your biggest fan, reaching for your star in my sky
One day, you'll look into the mix and notice me

I'm coming at you in 3D, broadcasting in
HD, full screen, crystal-clear clarity
Cheering the loudest for you to succeed continuously
You heard me, me, me cheering and clapping my hands
I'm sure you'll noticed me, me, your biggest fan

Hold Me?

Look at me for who I am and then
Look at me from time to time when
You think I'm who you thought I was not
My winters are cold too, and my summers are hot

You look to me, and I appear unshaken by the thunderstorm
You look to me when you're freezing so
my body can keep you warm
In me, you'll find some things that I have forgot
In me, you'll find that I've been measured and weighed a lot

Come to me from time to time then
Come to me for who I am when
You need someone in which you can depend
To measure twice and cut once before I weigh in

Know that a mountain crumbles and rocks do slide
Know that, without the wind beneath an
eagle's wings, it could not glide
If you would, even when I look strong, would you hold me
If you could, even then, every now and again, could you hold me

There's Always Room

Is that peanut butter and jelly? I got the bread
Two glasses of low-fat milk straight to the head
Is that a jelly doughnut? Let me fill the hole
Ain't nothing like hot dripping jelly when the day is so cold

Look at those hot pancakes; I'll cover them in maple syrup
With fresh strawberries, I'd just burp and slurp
Um, bacon and eggs between toasted bread
I'll add a sausage link in a blink and some sandwich spread

Is that a sweet peach in bowl of cream
It must be heaven-sent; this must be a dream
Do cherries grow on trees or on a cherry bush
I know the answer; you must pull the stem, not push

I'm hungry; it seems as if I haven't ate
I long for just a little more, a little on my plate
No matter how much I eat, there's one thing I do know
If there's no room for a tall glass of water,
there's always room for Jell-O

My First Toy

My first toy or last
I heard the maker broke the mold, then throw away the cast
It's probably not the only one made, but it is one of a kind
It may be duplicated, but if you look closer, the original is mine

My first toy or last
All I can do is smile while reflecting on my past
We can play with my toy day and night
My toy, when it burst, it elicits delight

My first toy or last
Time flies by way too fast
We can play with my toy; we're both grown
My toy explodes when heated or blown

My first toy or last
Anyhoo, let's play with my toy; we'll have a blast
We can play with my toy; it's loads of fun
Cowboys and Indians, cops and robbers, all have on

Coarse Course

I'm winning the race, but I may as well be blind
I've not taken the time to take a look around or behind
The coarse course of life is littered with a world of splendor
If I've missed out, how could I consider myself a winner

My race is a race against the hands of time
It's gaining on me, and it will claim what I consider mine
I've gathered meaningless possessions along the way
The weight of it all has slowed my pace day after day

Gray hairs like winter's snow, they remind me of the season
Young to old, I race headlong; I can't think of a good reason
I've missed so much in life by being on the go
Time has kept its steady pace; but me, me, I've begun to slow

I've lost my pace with time; I've run so long I've lost my mind
I'm walking this race now to enjoy the splendors I find
Love of family and friends is all I need in this race against time
I'm winning, so I'll take my time and walk across the finish line

On Top of It All

No words of fame or glory
A word, hell or purgatory
One tale to tell is a true story
It's a damn shame, and for that, I'm truly sorry

More is the price demanded upon those with the least to give
On top of it all is where gluttonous desire grows and lives
Dirty hands feed greasy mouths gravy and fat
No leftovers, no scraps, none of this nor a morsel of that

On the top of it all, overlooking the great fall
Standing on the backs of those consider useless and small
Some kill, others steal, and a few sell their souls
Gold and money, fermented greed's goals

On top of it all, the view downward and upward gets steeper
The climb to the top of it all left behind, out of mind, the weaker
Cries for relief, eyes filled with grief, unseen, unheard
Hell or purgatory, a word

The One That Got Away

No one will believe me, but that's okay
Somebody needs to know about the one that got away
Hunters strategize on how to catch the prefect prey
Me, me, I'm not a big-game hunter per se

My hook was dapperly baited; it had that come-get-me look
My plan was no plan, so don't fret; it was all by the book
I was sitting on the boat, waiting patiently
To cast my reel into the deepness of the sea

I got several hits, and then I got a bite
I knew this was the one I've been waiting for all night
I could tell by the way it bent my rod; I was in for a good fight
It tugged, and I tugged from left to right; we
tugged until it was nice and tight

Soak and wet, in and out, a few minutes, a few hours expire
It won't let go of my taunt wire; and me, me, I would not tire
I could feel it coming to a head; it was long overdue
My rod exploded; it snapped back into the deep blue

In My Eyes

I want to take a look around and walk inside
Don't blink; don't close your eyes; there's no reason to hide
When I walk in yours, you, you walk into mine
Watch that first step on your journey into my mind

Everything is as it seems to be until you take a closer look
Judge the cover if you dare; you may want to read the book
An escort will guide you through this labyrinth of time and age
Follow closely the navigator and keep your
limbs and head within the safety cage

All my skeletons are in the garden, helping my roses grow
Blood warms only in my heart; my mind,
it's a blizzard, colder than any snow
Winter gear will be provided on your journey to each pole
Like an iced-over ocean, my mind and my
story are littered with numerous holes

Will you open up so that I might take a journey to the other side
My mind is overcrowded, and there is nowhere for me to hide
You're welcome to come in here, where no one hears your cries
Be careful not to look to deep or too long
into these brown or hazel eye

Thought Omelet

Think'n and look'n at a pack of cigarettes with my omelet
Think'n of things not thought of yet
Think'n of the whys and why nots of a sure bet
Think'n why can't one be, but one of two is a set
Think'n 'bout what I do and what I don't regret
Think'n, if I could, I would think to forget

Think'n should I have one now or depart quickly or jet
Think'n how can one receive and leave and still get
Think'n whether I can allow and release; I mean let
Think'n of all those whom I have and I have not met
Think'n of rubbing on one and having one is the same as pet
Think'n of the ways I can without swimming in the water to get wet

Think'n time and experience are but age
doesn't make a doctor or vet
Think'n that the wicked web one weaves is a catcher's or fisher's net
Think'n of the pain enjoyed and the joy of pain are pleasures beset
Think'n, if one doesn't start, one won't have to quit nor fret
Think'n that my thoughts are mixed over a pack of cigarettes
Think'n my thoughts are the eggs of my thought omelet

Control Alt Delete

For every right, there is a wrong
For every occasion, there is a song
For every up, there is a down
For every broken wheel, there's a merry-go-round

Nothing in life but love should be deep seeded
Jealousy, distrust, and hate should be deleted
I can't control the weather, be it dark or clear skies
Who controls the rain clouds that form in one's eyes

Am I the yoke on your neck, the shackles on your feet
Am I an alternate in an unfulfilled dream? Am I bittersweet
Mistakes are made, and lessons are learned
Fire and passion are heated pleasures until one gets burned

For every right, there is a wrong
For every occasion, there is a song
Fouls, errors, and flaws plague us all; they're our lesser feats
Forgive but never forget to reboot the love; hit control, alt, delete

How Am I Doing

I'm doing well
I'm surviving the pains and pleasures of trying
my best not to be dragged to hell
Every now and again, I have to remind
myself that my soul is not for sale
I'm plagued by unchecked thoughts and a never-
ending hunger for things I dare not tell

One step forward and two steps back, I've
slipped and wobbled, but I've not fell
I've not yet heard the toll of the bell
I'm not confined to a room with bars, nor
is my mind without a brain cell
I'm so happy about living this life…can't you hear me yell

Up roaring emotions, battling good intentions
and bad notions, I've managed to quell
I'm alone in thought but not in life, so in
between here and there, I dwell
I'm taking life a day at a time; the fresh flowers, yes, I do smell
If you didn't know, now you know; I'm over
and under a bad and a good spell

I'm moving in slow motion like a snail, but my mind is snell
I've taken to listening to the ocean through a seashell
Wave after wave, they're trying to wash away
my sure shores; but all in all, I'm swell
Anyhoo, like I was saying, I'm doing well in the mell

Tell Me Why

The red rooster crossed the road to get to the other side
The long-neck ostrich stuck its head in the ground in order to hide
Now that I've answered those age-old questions about this and that
Tell me why my dog loves to chase after your cat

Why do salmon swim across the ocean into
a stream just to breed and die
Why is this urge so strong? Me, me, I often wonder why
All other thoughts suppress themselves
before I have a chance to realize
I've crossed the road like the red rooster getting to the other side

Like the long-neck ostrich, I want to stick
my head in but not in order to hide
Why don't penguins fly? Like them, I also love to slip and slide
Before it's all said and done and right before it is too late
Most living organisms will attempt to while others will copulate

I wish I could talk about it and call it by its name
Like the dog chases the cat, me, me, I'm without shame
The red rooster crossed the road to get to the other side
The long-neck ostrich stuck its head in the ground in order to hide

The Letter Never Sent

Thank you for all you've done for me
I appreciate your time and sincerity
You believed in me when I did nothing good
You believed in me when I didn't and I should

I reflect upon us and the days gone by
Good and not-so-good times bring a tear or two to my right eye
My voice breaks a little as I vocalize
Still waters run deep, but not as deep as the love between you and I

Alone in my thoughts, and it's of you I think
Breaking bread as we share a toast a drink
Blood, sweat, and tears, I've thought to document
The letter is imprinted with my soul-bound sacrament

It's been weighed and measured, its postage
due; I've paid in full like rent
I'm sending this letter, special delivery, alone
with loving memories of time well spent
Encapsulated is the splendor so relevant it's eloquent
The letter never sent

To Sum It Up

If I knew then what I know now
The milk is free, so why buy the cow
At the end of the rainbow, there's a pot of gold
At the end of the road, nothing's bought or sold

If I could, I'd like to sum it up
I'd prefer the water first, then the wine in my cup
The blacker the berry, the sweeter the juice
Youth is a bitter grape; mature grapes are wild and loose

A want is a nicety, and if compounded, it's greed
A lack is to be without seeds to sow in a bed of need
A stitch in time could patch a hole in all of mine
Sought by all is a piece of mind; if I seek, I'm sure I'll find

Life is sweet as a chocolate peanut butter cup
Left up to me, I'd like to sum it up
If I knew now what I should have known then
To sum it up, I'd do it a little different, but I'd one mo' gin

A Little Relief

Have you thought about the heat of the
day, burning desire and/or grief
Have you thought of a way to get a little relief
Have you thought of how easily the heart
is stolen by a charming thief
Have you heard the Queen of Hearts? She ran away with
the Jack of All Trades; that's all I'll say to be brief
They played in the heat of the day and at night…
um, they got a little more than relief
Play the cards and the hand you're dealt
Express those loving feelings as they're felt
It's better to have loved than not to have loved at all
Gravity shows it best: everything that goes up will, in time, fall
Due to the weight of it all
Down by the cherry tree, where what's in a name first showed it me
It was hairy and black, she called it a cat;
well, it looked like a manhole to me
So I erected my utility pole deep into her
manhole down by the cherry tree
Where knowledge and relief were gained
by what's in a name and me
Show and tell is a game we play known to placate curiosity
You say curiosity killed the cat?
A quest for knowledge? I don't believe that
It had to be the heat, the burning desire and/or the grief
Or it may have been the thief getting more than a little relief

She Loves Me, She Loves Me Not

One each to the other, we don't ask for a lot
She likes it with cream and sugar; I like it black and hot
She all but asked me to sleep in that, you know, the sweet spot
She loves me; she loves me not

On my side of the sheets, there she so beautifully lies
What do I say, as I caress her creamy thighs
and look in her dreamy eyes
The bed, unlike the sidewalk, I'd walk
closest to traffic nearest the street
Shouldn't she protect me from the bedding and the sheets

How did this happen? What do I have to lose
What are the rules from which I can choose
If I must take aim at this issue, I'll have this one shot
She loves me; she loves me not

If only I could phone a friend to ask why not
I've enjoyed our moments from beginning to end, so why stop
Do I or don't I sleep soundly in that specially made wet spot
She loves me; she loves me not

I Didn't Write It Down

I woke up midmorning with one thought
on my mind and void of time
Birds were singing love songs, and the
soft sun simply shone its shine
The most marvelously majestic memorable moment mesmerized me
I woke up early this morning, I mean late this
midmorning, with eyes wide open to see

I step through the mirror, and now I understand the other side
I ate the fruit and drank the juice; I'm drunk off life; get in; I'll drive
I peeled back every layer of the onion, and there are no more tears
I counted the rings of the redwood, and
age is a blessing, nothing to fear

I was naked as a jaybird and proud as a lion is of its mane
As I woke this evening, I mean this morning, nothing was the same
I woke last night—I mean midmorning,
not this afternoon—to the sounds
The world isn't as heavy as it was before or
after we rode life's merry-go-round

I've awaken to a new day, and I didn't write it down
I'm not sure when I woke up, but I'm sure of the sound
I've been ridiculously meticulous when it comes to the whys of how
I heard lovebirds copulating during the intercourse
of our I'll-always-love-you vows

C'est La Vie
(Say La Vee)

That's life or such is life, say la vee
If one ain't making life do what it does, so
one can do what one must do
Life will have its way with you, and justice
is not always the justice due
Open eyes wide that are open wide shut to life's unsolved mysteries
'Twas blinded by the light; 'twas blind, but now eye see
That's life or such is life, say la vee
Day breaks away from the twilight
What's done in the dark will come to light
Calm predates the impending trials of a temperate, turbulent storm
Perplexing is the perpetual cycle, so beware of being lukewarm
That's life or such is life, say la vee
Tomorrow is only a day away
Today hastens into yesterday
A clock keeps time like an open cage keeps a ravenous beast
Time escapes the clock, and on all of us, it does feast
That's life or such is life, say la vee
Proper planning prevents piss-poor performance
Preparation and practice prepare we, the pugilist, for the big dance
If you fail to plan, you have planned to fail;
life's a close call or a close shave
Predestined is a destiny or a destination on
a road paved to an untimely grave
That's life or such is life, say la vee

What Do I Want to Be

When I grow up, what do I want to be
I want to be an old, mighty oak tree
I want to weather the storms on land and on the high seas
I want to cast a shadow and shelter all who seek comfort in me

When I grow up, I want to be the color red
Fire and flame, burning hot as I spread
Red and yellow will kill a fellow dead
Freedom's price is steep, and deep is the blood bled

When I grow up, I want to be young and old instead
Too soon, I've outgrown the cradle but not the bed
I want to be a roller coaster even though I'd be a better sled
Unleavened or without yeast is what I'd be if I could be bread

When I grow up, I want to be king of the
four seasons, winter through spring
I want to be one, not two of everything
I've never really thought about being anything other than me
When I grow up, what do I want to be

Away

Who's driving anyway? I'd prefer the highway
Turn left for a quick getaway
U-turns have the right-of-way
Ignore the red lights on the freeway
Pay all fines due now or later or by the way
Every driver has to pull into a driveway
To rest in a hideaway
Conductor, please, I don't want to take the subway
I'm trying to stay on the right side of the railway
Who's driving, and I need to know straightaway
Calgon, take me away; I'm going to make away
To make life do what it does, I will find away
Life without risk, know there's no safe way
Yesterday fades away, and tomorrow is always a day away

Deadlines

The clock is ticking off the seconds, minutes, and hours
It can't be slowed or stopped by any source or power
Step by step, we're hand in hand; it keeps me company
We've both aged, but I've noticed time has taken a toll on only me

We've spent our springs sightseeing in youthful bliss
Our summers, we ran wild in heat and did things I'll not list
Our autumns, we'd look back and reminisce on it all
Our winters, I think time was better spent in the fall

Yes, time has seasoned me as it ought
It's priceless; most think that it can be bought
Time is actually older than dirt
Time loves no one, and with all of us, time flirts

We have gotten to know one and another along the way
I've learned it's not the destination or the journey per se
From–to, Alpha–Omega, the beginning and end of time
It is how one spends each moment between the deadline

I Can Do Anything

I was told I can do anything as long as I try
I never believed it because all I wanted to do was fly
Like Superman, I took three steps and jumped to no avail
I tried every day and every night without fail

I practiced on rooftops…nonstop
Like a high jumper, I did the Fosbury Flop
I climbed the highest tree to study the birds
I thought, if I chirped, the birds would spread the word

They would not reveal their secret of flight to me
So I took to lying in flower beds to consult with the bumblebees
They told me scientist said they should not be able to fly
They told me not to be discouraged and to continue to try

I drove to the airport as I considered my plight
(Between you and me, I'm afraid of heights)
I purchased a ticket on the earliest flight
I was told I can do anything as long as I try
I never believed it because all I wanted to do was fly

They Asked Me

They asked me who I thought I was
I told them I am me; I make life do what it does
They asked me why I wasn't more like them
I told them that a rock is just a stone and I'm a precious gem
They asked me why haters hate and how do I do the things I do
I told them I love me some me; try loving you some you
They asked me how to love and where should they begin
I told them to banish self-loathing; it's a disease that starts within

They asked me what it takes to be a man
I told them the jury was still out; it up for debate
but to take their responsibilities hand in hand
They asked me from what book they should read day and night
I told them to read from the book which shows
them how to walk by faith and not by sight
They asked me what's the most important story ever to be told
I told them it is the story of how they learned to play their role
They asked me have they come to the dinner too late
I told them everyone who sits at the table to eat won't get a plate

Wish for Fish

All my life, I've had to fight…these eagers of delight
I've just tried to do things right
I want to go deep in her wetness all night
For my sore eyes, she's a hell of a sight

If I had one wish, I'd ask for a lifetime
To spend all my pennies in exchange for this dime
We would never have to share a word
I hear her loud and clear, and here's what I heard

She said, "Poppy, whatever you want, I'll
give you whatever you need
"My voluptuous tulip is your garden.
Please fertilize it with your seed"
Me, me, I'm only human; and this cat brings out the dog in me
She's not the last cat on a hot tin roof, but
that pussy is worth a look-see

All my life, I've had to fight…
I've just tried to do things right
I said all that to say this, if I could have but one wish
I know there's always room for Jell-O; I wish I had room for her fish

Santa Died

It was the night before Christmas, and the trap was set
I sat out milk and cookies, then armed myself, so don't fret
This was my first investigation as a nongovernmental spy
I intended on capturing this burglar who
left gifts; I knew it was a lie

Breaking and entering and stealing a meal to some isn't a big deal
But to me, a crime was being committed
every year, and that's for real
I wasn't trying to be a hero, but I am who I am
I knew in my heart that children worldwide
would thank me for ending this scam

With no chimney, the bandit had to enter the front or back door
On Christmas day, I planned to end this crime spree forevermore
No one but me knew of my heroic plot or
the impact of my historic deed
I would capture this prolific criminal by feeding his insatiable greed

Everyone was asleep and snuggled tightly in their beds
Me, me, I lay in wait instead; I had to
capture a bandit dressed in all-red
The capture didn't go as I had planned because
I really wanted to take him alive
We were face-to-face and eye to eye; it was he
or I; read my report on how I survive

Need I Say It

Should I tell you each and every day
What are the three words you'd like most for me to say
I've been told I should, but I hear that's hearsay
This can't be used as a matter of fact per se

I said it more than once or twice, and we've shared a smile
I admit I enjoyed it, so maybe I haven't said it in a while
The sun rises and sets on a sky so beautifully blue
Day and night, the sun's light radiates from you

From every coast to every shore of many distant lands
Our hourglass is never empty; we have plenty of sand
From the top of the mountains to the depths of the seas
Latitude and longitude, our love can't be measured in degrees

Words build and destroy; they convolute and persuade
The wrong or right words could rain on our mayday parade
We're in life's race together where actions and words keep us fit
Before, during, or after the race, need I say it

Under the Rainbow

It's under the rainbow, so stand by the phone and wait for my call
There's a picture of a rainbow hanging on a wall
Now at the end of the rainbow, there is a pot
Now don't lift the lid; I'm not sure if it is filled or not

What you have to ask yourself is on which wall
Where is the picture at, and when will he call
What kind of pot could it be
If I lift the lid, what will I see

Now the story would be best if you should find gold
But this picture hangs over a toilet bowl
Hide-and-seek is a game of hit or miss
First I need to go and take a much-needed piss

When I call, I want you to go down the
hall, and there you may find it
Lift the lid slow and hold your nose; it may be full of shit
But you'll never know until you find it
I'll call soon or in a minute

Happy with Me

I took all the pictures of myself, and I hid them out of sight
They reminded me of my past, and my
recollections of it weren't quite right
Some were so dark and blue while others were taken in a bad light
Not all of them were bad; those without me were brilliantly bright

Those pictures of me which I took down
displayed something I didn't like
Each one I reviewed to ameliorate (to improve) my
feelings of myself so deeply rooted within my psyche
Those pictures were marred reflections of who I was
I was unsure of my purpose then, so I did things just because
I dated each picture as I recalled the dash
between each date along the line
I carefully reflected on the dash, on each event, on each moment in time
I replaced the pictures with mirrors in order
for me to see exactly where I stand
I've had an arduous journey through life, from being lost to this
unmarked destination not found any map or located any land

After careful review, the pictures glowed and reflected so brilliantly bright
They illuminated my milestones; they marked
my way from the darkness into the light
I no longer need the pictures or the mirrors
for me to reflect or for me to see
Who I was or who I am, I'm happy with
me, the person I've ventured to be.

Sugar and I

Sugar and I, we got a taste for all things sweet
My mouth is watering, and mind is thinking of delicious treats
Diabetes or Sugar told me I have to monitor what I eat
My desires are driving me crazy, and I'm losing plenty of sleep
Cookie, Candy, Cake, and Ice Cream—we did
what's worth doing; we did our thing
They're so sweet; "Who Can Make the
Sunshine" is the song they love to sing
Sugar and I have a lifelong love; she gives me the
energy to fly above from here to there
She told me, in no uncertain terms, that
Carbohydrates and I must end our lurid affair
It's been difficult to end my relationships because
Cookie, Candy, Cake, and Ice Cream call me
I've changed my diet number, but they've
looked me up in the food directory
Most of the time, they phone from an unknown
number; and me, me, I answer the call
Day and night, my phone rings off the hook;
they're driving me up the wall
Sugar and I affirm and reaffirm our love at least twice a day
She assures, then reassures me, no matter how
high or how low, she'll love me always
Sugar and I, we got a taste for all things sweet
My mouth is watering, and mind is thinking of delicious treat

In the Land of Lack

It's all about how one chooses to live
From hand to mouth to having it all or in between take and give
If I could just pinch an inch, you better know I'd pinch off a mile
From rags to riches is an American dream; it's a lifestyle
I'm from the other side of the invisible yet divisible tracks
On one side, there's the land of milk and
honey; on my side, there's lack
The oven heats the house, and food stamps are traded like gold
WIC feeds my hunger; powdered milk
taints the water in my cereal bowl
For a new pair of shoes, I'd act a fool and wear
the soles out before the end of school
A ditch filled with water entertains me and keeps
me cool; it's my own private swimming pool
I looked up to the real moneymakers—thugs, pimps,
ballers, and even one time out on the take
Livin' large in the land of lack, pushing mad weight
while stacking and snacking on cheese and cake
I had my eyes on this prize until reality hit me like Ike hit Tina
Most of my friends have names ending in
life, *felony*, and my girl, *misdemeana*
All found dead on the tracks
A railroad signal is needed: train kills another from the land of lack

I've Been Told

I've been told not to rock the boat
I've often wondered, if it capsized, would it float
I've been told the squeaky wheel gets the oil
I've been boisterous, but there's no ease for my toil
I've been told a closed mouth doesn't get fed
I've been hungry for words left unsaid
I've been told there's nothing new under the sun
I've longed for original thoughts of what's
been and what's been left undone
I've been told to keep my head up to the sky
I've pondered drowning in misguided
pride as the world passes me by
I've been told to shoot for the moon, and if I missed, I'd hit the stars
I've done one better; I've set my sights on
a little red planet called Mars
I've been told love is a many splendid thing
I've witnessed its joy along with its broken
and its tarnished bands and rings
I've been told not to worry, for today eases
into tomorrow and into another day
I've often made a wish, for momma said there would
be day like this that I'd wish for yesterday

Friendship

Friendship is like a cruise ship that often perilously
sails through the uncharted waters of life
Our passengers and crew embark on this voyage
knowing there will be struggles and strife
We all laugh, we all cry, we all succeed, and sometimes we all fail
It's not the voyage we remember but the
experiences we encounter as we raised sails

At the pearly gates, the sign we read "From
which friendship do you hail"
Davey Jones's locker will be overflowing
with souls and stories of our tales
From ship to shore
Our friendship is forevermore

Still Fighting the War

I'm not afraid to fall asleep at night
I'm use(d) to waking up before, during, or after the fight
Cold sweats and my heart racing, I jump up, still in my bed
My only comfort comes in knowing it's all in my head
For twenty-two years, eleven months, and two
days, I practiced, I trained, and I rehearsed
I prepared to detect, to delay, and to destroy
our enemies in combat or worse
I stood on entry-point gates, patrolled inner
and outer perimeters in constant wait
I lay in foxholes, peeped through mouseholes,
looking and listening till this very date
Vanguard, Philippines, during political unrest
and right before Mount Pinatubo blew
Vanguard, Saudi Arabia, Khobar Towers bombed
and after our Twins fell one and two
Vanguard, France, guarding aircraft that watched
and took the fight from far in advance
Vanguard, Bosnia-Herzegovina genocide, after
Slobodan Milosevic stood his last stance
Vanguard, Afghanistan, conveys and thirteen air
combat support missions, what a fright
Fallen and wounded comrades and our
enemies, they visit with me at night

I'm retired from active duty, and yes, my
home has its own perimeter fence
I check it constantly as well as the roof, grounds,
doors, and windows—my first lines of defense
I stay armed and combat ready, and I sleep very light…
Excuse me…there…someone at my front door
Don't fret; I'm armed, I'm trained, and I'm well
rehearsed; I'm still fighting the war

Happy Anniversary of Your First Birth

Happy are the days you've lived to enjoy your footsteps
through the distant mile marks of life's years.
Your blessings are weighed by your good and bad
deeds; they're measured by your faith and delineated
by time shared with family and friends held dear.
You're born once from the water into life, and you're reborn in
the water and into the light, so you're born not once but twice.
I wish you a happy anniversary of your first birth, and may
your years be well seasoned by life's sugar and spice.
Happy anniversary in memory of your birth
and your time spent on earth.

Thank You for Giving

Thank you for giving of thee
Thank you for all you've done for me
Thank you for caring
Thank you for sharing

Thank you for giving of thee
Thank you for all you've done for we
Thank you for being more than a friend
Thank you for staying by us until the end

Thank you for giving of thee
Thank you for all you've done for me
Thank you for your time
Thank you for giving me peace of mind

Thank you for giving of thee
Thank you for all you've done for we
Thank you for wishing us the best of luck
Thank you for really giving a phuck

Bats in the Belfry

Built on solid sound, and me, me, I listen attentively
To the bells' informative chimes and rings,
and me, me, I compiled willingly
My clocks are set, and I place all my bets
on the meter, or so to speak
Like a bell tower, I'm head and feet; I'm measured from base to peak

I've not stopped to question what's being heard or said
Why have I not considered the direction or where I'm being led
Who's in the belfry making these insane pitches in my head
Only a few can interpret these notes as they crescendo in blood red

In my mind, there's a constant meter by which I'm bound
When I'm alone, I fill the space between
the positive and the ground
My thoughts are built on solid sound
Who's in the belfry making these noises and moving around

I dared not climb the tower to look inside, for the trebly is too high
Should I risk climbing up to see? No, I
might fall headlong into the sky
Float away on a note or drown in the noises if I don't try
I don't know, but I've been told there are bats in the belfry

A Man and His Dog

There was a man who questioned his pet
If you had hands, would you handle it and not lick it wet
If you had hands instead of paws
Wouldn't you dig with a shovel and not with your claws

If you had hands, wouldn't you clap
Wouldn't you love hearing your fingers pop and snap
Wouldn't you like to wave hello and goodbye
Wouldn't you swipe instead of scratching your eyes

Wouldn't you enjoy it more shaking hands
You could write down your thoughts and even your plans
Wouldn't you like to hold your young pups
You could give up those bowels for plates and cups

The dog answered without a word
The man listened attentively, and here's what he heard
"I love who I am. You're just another envious fan"
Lifting his back leg, he began licking it so
his master could understand
He was simply saying "Look at me, man, no hand"

Happy New Year

Over the river and through the woods, to Grandma's house we go
That song is a classic, it reminds us of no one we actually know
Let's think about the events that's brought us here
Through the good and the bad times, we've entered a new year

From springing forward to falling back
in time through rain and shine
The days and nights have bestowed upon us this moment in time
We've watched the clock tick off the wall
We've waited unwavering for the new year to give us call

When January rings, we'll answer by saying, "Happy New Year"
We'll all celebrate in our own way, and a few of us, we'll share a tear
January to December, 12 months, 365 days
Some of us crawled, others walked, and a
few of us ran a very long way

The new year has welcomed us all here
from the visionaries to the blind
Some will pray for world peace, and others
will pray for peace of mind
Happy New Year to you, you, and you; I pray
that, whatever you seek, you'll find
Happy New Year to one and to all; happy New Year to all mankind

Untitled

I was reading, and my ears got tired of hearing what my mouth had
to say, and my eyes seen words that mouth refused to utter anyway.
I closed my mouth and shut my eyes and paid
no attention to what I could not hear.
Then I saw things in my mind which left me to
wondering why aren't my eyes that keen and clear.

Was I dreaming about things I had but I had not seen?
It felt real to me, if you know what I mean.
When I woke, not a word I wrote, not a
sound I spoke, not a sight I've seen.
I lay there soaking wet with my heart
racing from thoughts or a dream.

So when I woke, I read words my mouth refused to
speak, and I heard words my ears could not hear.
I'm not afraid, yet my mind lives in perpetual fear.
When I close my eyes, I'll leave the lights on,
so y'all come back now…you hear.

I Believe in You

When times are hard and the light at the
end of the tunnel can't be seen
When no one understands your visions,
your aspirations, your dreams
When life shows you one thing, then you discover
life isn't what you thought or as it seems
When you've finally cross over the fence and
you find out that the grass isn't as green
I believe in you
When no one seems to understand your
visions, your aspirations, your dreams,
Will you allow me to be your comforter, your shelter from the cold
Can we walk hand in hand through the ups and
downs, one step at a time into the age of old
I believe in you
When life shows you one thing, then you realize
life isn't what you thought or as it seems
I'll stand fast; I'll be there for you for true
I'll support you wholeheartedly on your
path, your course, your avenue
When times are hard and the light at the
end of the tunnel can't be seen
When you finally cross over the fence only to
find out that the grass isn't as green
When you're in too deep, I'll be pulling harder than even you
Me, me, I believe in you

Life: No One Gets Out Alive

Life is more than the sum of its whole, yet it's
never been solved mathematically
Standing on the outside, looking in or on the
inside, looking out metaphorically
Life is a series of moments during a period,
overlooking the past and present tense
Divided by occurrences of like events, then
subtracted by all things of relevance

Life is more than a board game; we're all
born ignorant of the rules per se
There are as many strategies to win as
there are players waiting to play
There's a closely guarded secret known by gamers;
no gamer is awarded immortality
No player gets out of life alive in reality

Life is more than a card game; we're all
required to play the hands we're dealt
Each card played changes the name of the game
to feelings of missed chances greatly felt
There's a closely guarded secret known by card
players; aces are trumped by deuces wild

No player gets out of life alive, no man, no woman, no child
Life is more than a foot race; we're all born barefoot and fancy-free
Some runners pace themselves while others run all out furiously
There's a closely guarded secret known by
runners; the race run is hard on the soles
No runner finishes the race alive, and only a few
will win the gold and save their soul

There's a Time

There's a time when the chickens come home to roost
If you getting it how you live, pump your brakes
or accelerate to give your life a boost
There's a time when what's done in the dark will come to light
If you're ashamed about the things you're doing,
even a dimwit looks twice as bright

There's a time when the fat lady will sing
If you're not prepared, winter will be your season during the spring
There's a time when push comes to shove
If you're straddling the fence, you could fall in or out of love

There's a time when young birds must strengthen
their wings and leave the nest
If you fail to plan, then you plan to fail life's entire test
There's a time for all things big and tall
and those things short and small
If you pay what you owe, you may get some or none at all

There's a time for crying, lying, and dying
If you make life do what it does so you can do
what you do, your spirit will be high flying
There's a time when all good things must come to an end
If you're not taken care of your own business,
someone else will; ask your friend

You Got a Rise

Don't worry, it normally happens when I have to…
We both can agree it rises early or way before me
I know, to you, it appears to be a big deal
Two all-beef patty special sauce comes as a meal

Don't try it without any hands; stop her
Because it takes two hands to handle a whopper
I'd like a shake with those fries
Know one thing, girl, you got a rise

I was looking at your cherry pie
With ice cream on the side, oh my
My mouth is watering for that cherry and cream
You got a rise out of me, and what you see isn't a dream

Where's the beef? You better ask Wendy; she knows
You got a rise out of me, and it shows
Don't worry; yes, it's alive
You got me crazing and craving; yes, you got a rise

Slavery

I was hung at parties called picnics
I was forbidden to read or do arithmetic
I was sold and herded like cattle
I was the subject and a minor cause of an internal state war or battle
I was not a whole person and given a new name
I was taken from one land by ship in chains
I was raped; I was beaten; I was denied my density
I was killed at will, and justice saw it, but it didn't see

Time slipped into the future or presently
Master came out the big house and said we's free
Forty acres and a mule promised and never received
Equality under Jim Crow, we were not all deceived
On the fourth of July, we pop firecracker as if we were free
That's the date Willy Lynch came to America
with rope for the hanging tree
Slavery has not died; believe this; the devil is liar
Prisons are the new slave quarters, and the
breeding ground for the invisible empire

Paid in Blood

Over the course of several tears, I've noted
I've just taken time out and wrote it
A check that will not bounce
Measured in grams or by the ounce
Over mountains and through valleys, life's highs and lows
You've been there with your tickets for every show
Featuring me riding dirty and flamed up on the come up
I flipped a one-eighty and phucked the script up
I signed my name in the space allotted four times
Questions I never asked, like why I was
paid to put my life on the line
I did it for free on them blocks while bending
corner in them big city streets
The grind made more cheddar, and life was bittersweet
Me, me, I'm standing here in the mirror,
looking at no one else but you
You do want to get paid how you live, don't you
I wrote your check, dripping with blood
from here at home to distant lands
Duty, honor, country scrawled with blood-soaked hand

I'm Not in Here

I'm not in here
Me and Myself, who do they fear
I, I, I'm afraid of Me and Myself; I'm not in here
Life is a dance I does while Me and Myself observe others who dare
To glance, to look, or to stare
I feel misunderstood by all who are concerned
I'm even less understood by those who have taken
time with I and claim to have learned
I'm lost in this labyrinth of known and unknown paths,
roads, two-way streets, and lonely highways
In then out of step, with life's measured
steps, calculated using slide rulers
While I's sickle reaps what's abandoned by Me and Myself's days
I'm scared to step backward or forward; yes, I'm
very afraid in here deep within My's mind
The sky is falling, and the clocks in My's
world have lost track of time
Day dances the two-step shuffle with Night, while every
step taken by Darkness is illuminated by Light
I have struggled to learn life's two steps while Me and
Myself doubted whether I even know left from right
I'm not in here; I'm alone in thought
Me and Myself are afraid of I, and for good reason, they ought
Me and Myself doubt I, who is misunderstood and feared
Me and Myself left I alone, and I'm not in here

What Was I Talking About?

I never learned how to knit, crochet, or sew
I've forgotten more than I've thought to know
I learned to rip, to shred, and to tear through
Destroying everything old, used, and new
I never burned any bridges; I've crushed
crossing over from there to here to now
I meant to water and feed the mule that died
tilling my way with an anchor for a plow
Deeply rooted in self-destruction is where
the explosives flowers bud and grow
My mind is filled like an unmapped minefield
marked "Watch your next thought," oh no!
My wisdom teeth have been ripped from my mouth
My tongue licks at words that foolishly escape
from the north for freedom in the south
Don't convict me of caring; don't accuse me
sharing; don't judge me while the jury is out
I have blood on my hands from the dead, and my
gun shot the bullets known as reasonable doubt
My clothes are torn, my heart is worn, and my life is in need of repair
I have a head cold from thinking about fresh air
I could fix anything, but I never learned how to knit, crochet, or sow
What was I talking about? I've forgotten
more than I've thought to know

In My Short While

Me, me, I've not done a lot of things in my short while
I don't remember my first breath, my first step, my first smile
I was told I crawled backward before I crawled forward
I cried and laughed; I walked and ran; I
slept and played with my steward
Time has aged, matured, and weathered all but itself
Sugar, pressed fruit, and water ferment on a shelf
Time makes wine of us, and I'm ready for the wine-tasting test
I'm a diabetic with high sugar; I'm a mental basket
with fresh fruit, and I know I'm a nut; I'm a watered-
down version of life's worst at its best
In my short while, I've not remembered every moment of any day
I recall my hair was brownish red, but now it's black and gray
I'm still fermenting and growing stronger and
more intoxicating the longer I stay
I pray the grim reaper is not drunk; I'd hate
to be mistaken as ripe wheat or hay
In my short while, I've done what's made me, me;
and I've done it gangster, OG…and that's a fact
Insecure, afraid, scared, and even mortified, I
shook off haters like water off a duck's back
In my short while, time has taught, time has stalked,
and time has shown me its so-what-you-gonna-do
frown and its envious so-now-what smile
In my short while, I've not done a lot of things; but me,
me, I've walked barefoot down life's cobblestone mile

Coffee Break

When I sat at life's table, I came alone
Since I've come here, I've done plenty of wrong
There's an empty and full cup sitting on a coffee table
The full cup, I pour as much into it as I can until it is unable

To hold another drop and it overflows the rim
I love my life wet, hot, and dark, yes, dripping over the brim
Sugar and cream are simple pleasures had every now and again
The empty cup, I never use; I've set it out for a friend

My coffee break has lasted hours too long
I sit at the coffee table of life all alone
Sipping from this cup filled with just one more sin
Smiling faces tell lies, and liars, they just grin

Wide awake, I sit here sipping coffee at life's table
The full cup, I pour as much into it as I can until it is unable
To hold any right, when I've sipped the last drop of life's wrongs
I'll end my coffee break, and I'll leave alone

Those Eyes

It happened in a glance
It happened by what is known as chance
A sparkle shown in those eyes sparked desire
In these eyes and between those eyes, there burns a fire

Fueled by unchecked, unadulterated, unclothed, or naked passion
Those eyes cut like a knife through useless babble and hesitation
Those eyes ran up and down and approach from every angle
Those eyes and these eyes romanced and danced the dirty tango

Those eyes whispered sweet nothings but not in my ear
Those eyes opened these eyes to things eyes see but don't hear
Those eyes welcomed these eyes into a world of pleasure
These eyes accepted the invitation in every degree and measure

Those eyes pierced my hard, cold heart, if the story be told
Those eyes promised these eyes our romance would never grow old
Without a word said and after an eye dance, it happened in a glance
Those eyes and these eyes sparked a raging
fire that set off an explosive romance

Your Kiss

I wish I could sip
The moisture of morning dew from your lips
I'd quench my thirst from them as I grip
Your harmonious hypno'c hips
I wish…for the comfort of your voice
Telling me and the world I'm your choice
I wish…to be wrapped in your arms
To feel your warmth and bask in your charms
I wish I could make love to you in every way
I'd love you night and day
I wish I didn't have to wish for what I don't want to sorely miss
I wish…for your kiss

Just Do It Right

What do you call a lizard without any legs
What good is a chicken that doesn't lay eggs
Now, either you know the answers, or you don't
I was going to tell you, but now, now I won't

If life were as simple as I've led you to believe
Have another fig and grab a few more leaves
Shame and pride were born from lies
Deception and deceit cry for the truth as the truth dies

While you sit here under this tree, eating all you can
Filling your belly with the food man and
Wonder what's the promise made to you
You're of this world, and this world is of you too

As the lizard climbed down out the tree, then lost its legs
Three days was the resurrection, and the pagan
Easter Bunny ran off with the eggs
Live by faith and not by sight
Fill your belly with the word of the Lord, and
whatever you do, just do it right

As U Say

I'll do as u say
U can have it ur way
I won't show u the love inside
My passion I'll simply hide
I'll miss tasting u
I'll miss being deep within u
I'll miss holding u tight
I'll miss loving u, wrong or right
I'll do as u wish
Ur loving is what I'll miss
For u, I'll do anything at all
U've got my heart and loving on call
I'll do as u say
U can have it ur way
My love I'll keep bound and tied
My passion I'll simply hide

All We've Been Through

All we've been through
It seems like the more we can do
All we've been through
It's brought me closer to you
When we hold one another
We share a love like great lovers
You and I become one
We make romance and love fun
All we've been through
The more we will do
Our time has not run out
Our love, there is no doubt
You and I
We are no lie
All we've been through has been a test for true
It's brought me closer to you

Gather Mine

Don't play with my emotions
Don't rock the boat in the middle of the ocean
Don't check my pockets for your next success
Don't play with my paper don't create a grave mess
If you can't figure it, outside of my pockets
What you need to do is kick rocks, yes, drop it
Money maybe at the root of all evil
You dig up my roots you'll also see dead people
Everyone must pay their dues
Keeping what's mine know you'll lose
Playing games with my emotions is like playing with pocket change
From zero to superhero, I get real strange
Don't play with my emotions
Pay your dues, if not on time, then in time
Gather up mine

Keep living, and you'll see.

About the Author

Kevin Anderson

From ghetto fabulous to military standards with customs and courtesies. The Path taken in life from the United States of America to far and distant lands has indubitably exposed me bare. The adventure has made the person, the man. Born in Illinois, raised in East St. Louis and Royal Lakes, from there the fam hightailed it to California. Dallied in Inglewood then Bompton or Compton, some do say. Signed my name on the dotted line bringing world into full view. I joined the United States Air Force in 1986, fully retired in 2016, 30 years honorable service and of making life do what it does so I can do what I do when I do what I do communicating my thoughts or a few.

www.ingramcontent.com/pod-product-compliance
Lightning Source LLC
Chambersburg PA
CBHW020433130626
46549CB00001B/117